ORIGINS OF FESTIVALS AND FEASTS

ORIGINS OF FESTIVALS AND FEASTS

JEAN HARROWVEN

LINE DRAWINGS
by
LEN STRASMAN

PRYOR PUBLICATIONS
WHITSTABLE, WALSALL & WINCHESTER

PRYOR PUBLICATIONS
WHITSTABLE, WALSALL
AND WINCHESTER

© 1996 PRYOR PUBLICATIONS
75 Dargate Road, Yorkletts, Whitstable,
Kent CT5 3AE, England.
Tel. & Fax: (01227) 274655

Specialist in Facsimile Reproductions

First published in Great Britain by
Kaye & Ward Ltd.
1980

A CIP Record for this book is available from the British Library.

© Jean Harrowven

ISBN 09 46014 50 1

Printed and bound in England by
Biddles Ltd.

Woodbridge Park Estate,
Woodbridge Road,
Guildford GU1 1DA.

CONTENTS

Introduction

ST VALENTINE'S DAY   1

Valentine Buns, Valentine Cards

SHROVETIDE   8

The Pancake Bell, Pancake Competitions,
Sports and Games, Things for Children To Do

MOTHERING SUNDAY   24

Recipes For Children To Try, Gifts

EASTER   29

Maundy Thursday, Good Friday,
Games, Easter Sunday, Easter Monday,
Easter Customs, Recipes, Things For Children
To Do, Games

APRIL FOOLS' DAY   54

MAY DAY   60

Things For Children To Do

WHITSUNTIDE   69

Things For Children To Do

HARVEST   74

Things For Children To Do

HALLOWE'EN   81

Spells and Charms, Games,
Recipes, Things For Children To Make

GUY FAWKES DAY   99

Bonfires, The Guys, Food For Bonfire Night,
Fireworks, Bonfire Boys, Recipes, Things
For Children To Do

CHRISTMAS   128

Advent, St Nicholas and Santa Claus,
Christmas Carols, Wassailing, Christmas
Eve, Christmas Day, Boxing Day, Sports
and Games, Evergreens, Nature Customs,
Miracle and Mummers' Plays, Christmas
Crackers, Recipes, Things For Children To
Make, Christmas Cards, Christmas Card Verses,
Nativity Scenes

NEW YEAR'S EVE — HOGMANAY   173

AUTHOR'S ACKNOWLEDGEMENTS   178

BIBLIOGRAPHY   179-180

Old Customs! Oh I love the sound,
However simple they may be:
What e'er with time hath sanction found,
Is welcome and is dear to me.
Pride grows above simplicity
And spurns them from her haughty
mind,
And soon the poet's song will be
The only refuge they can find.

John Clare

INTRODUCTION

Long ago feasts and festivals were highlights in the lives of commoners. With the coming of Christianity the seasonal pagan celebrations were merged where possible with saint days to produce holidays which were approved by all. British festivals as so rightly explained by A.R. Wright and T.E. Lones, editors of *British Calendar Customs* are divided into two groups — movable and fixed festivals. The movable festivals such as Pancake Day and Easter do not have a fixed date on the calendar, whereas the festivals such as Guy Fawkes Day and Christmas Day are repeated annually on the same date.

Up to the middle of the last century there were at least 40 saint days in the year although not all of these were a public holiday. The lesser known saints were observed more locally than nationally and so people were given holidays at different times depending on which part of the country they lived in and the type of employment in which they were engaged. For example the lace makers celebrated the memory of their patron, St Catherine, on 25 November with a very enjoyable holiday. By the beginning of the nineteenth century some celebrations had deteriorated into rough brawls and the puritanical minded Victorians abolished many festivals and generally tidied up the public holidays. They had a passion for work and thought it uneconomical that the workers should be allowed so much free time. Later, paid holidays for a week at a time were introduced to replace the lost Bank holidays.

Up to 1830 the Bank of England closed on all 40 saint days but it was not until 1871 that Bank holidays were made lawful, through the work of Sir John Lubbock, and the government and the monarch stipulated which days should be official Bank holidays. In modern times, Good Friday, Easter Monday, the Spring Bank Holiday, replacing Whit Monday, August Bank Holiday, now changed to the last Monday in August, Christmas Day and Boxing Day are all Bank holidays and in addition in recent years we have New Year's day and the first Monday in May. In Scotland there are some differences — the first two days in the year are Bank holidays but Easter Monday is not and although Christmas Day is recognised, Boxing Day is not a holiday.

The monarch has the power to proclaim with the approval of parliament any extra days that she or he may think fit. And so we had another national holiday in Silver Jubilee Year — 6 June 1977 — an event that caught the imagination and good humour of the British nation.

Nowadays people tend to a large extent to forget why they have a Bank holiday but enjoy it without asking too many questions. Only a few of the pastimes and games associated with past holidays still exist. The marble competition held on Good Friday at Tinsley Green, Sussex is one that I do not think will die out, and the burning of guys on 5 November is just as popular as ever. Other games I have mentioned in this book may appeal to you and,I hope, enjoy a revival. Traditional foods such as Hot Cross Buns and Christmas cakes are obviously here to stay and I hope that other recipes that I have included will be tried out once more. Perhaps some of these ideas will be passed onto the younger generation — for what better way to preserve our traditions than through our children?

Now, in the age of computers we can look forward to more leisure, more pastimes, more relaxation and more fun. New interests will be introduced or revived. There may be more national holidays in the future and with this in mind a fresh community spirit will, hopefully, emerge so that once again we can experience the revels and gaiety of long ago.

Jean Harrowven
Norwich.

ST VALENTINE'S DAY —
14 FEBRUARY

It may come as a surprise to some of us that St Valentine was not the patron saint of lovers but the festival that we celebrate is in fact, like so many others, a combination of a pagan ritual and a Christian tradition.

St Valentine was a holy priest living in Rome in the third century, under the emperor Claudius Gothicus. In those days it was regarded as good sport by the authorities to round up practising Christians and either throw them to the lions or murder them in other ways. During a religious purge, Valentine and his friend Maurius helped Christians flee the city to the comparative safety of the countryside. Alas, Valentine was captured, and tortured to make him renounce his faith, but he did not succumb and was finally clubbed to death and then beheaded on 14 February AD 273.

Later, Pope Julius built a church to commemorate the memory of the martyred saint near Ponte Mole, and a gate at this city bore the name Porta Valentinni. It was later changed to Porta del Popolo. However the relics of St Valentine lie, so it is said, in the church of St Praxedes, Rome. Thereafter the illustrious martyr is mentioned many times in chronicles, including the writings of our own Venerable Bede.

The pagan festival of Lupercalia was celebrated on 15 February by young Romans, centuries before Christ. The celebration was held in honour of the goddess Februata Juno, and concerned all young people of marriageable age. The names or tokens representing all the young girls in the district were placed in a love urn, and the young lads each drew a token and the couples paired off. This was a kind of mating lottery game, and must have produced enormous excitement amongst the younger generation!

During the Roman occupation of Britain the idea was

brought to this country and was adopted by the ancient Britons. When people were converted to Christianity the pagan and Christian festivals were merged; therefore the festival of Lupercalia was put back a day and celebrated on St Valentine's day — 14 February. The old pagan customs still continued and in Britain up to the beginning of the present century it was customary for local lads and lasses to draw lots for partners. In Lancashire, for instance, on St Valentine's eve, the names of eligible young people were written on separate slips of paper and divided into two groups, male and female. The boys drew a slip from the girls' pile and vice versa. Thus each person received two sweethearts and then had to work out for themselves the most satisfactory arrangement. After the final selection had been made the swains treated their maidens to all sorts of outings and surprises including dances and gifts.

According to ancient custom 14 February was supposed to be the day the birds mated, and in fact it is now known that many birds do mate around this time. An old verse from Oxfordshire reminds us of this:

> *You'll be mine and I'll be thine,*
> *And so good-morrow Valentine,*
> *As I sat in my garden chair,*
> *I saw two birds fly in the air,*
> *And two by two and pair by pair*
> *Which made me think of you, my dear.*

The traditional rhymes associated with Valentine cards are much older than the actual cards. They were spoken when a gift was bestowed on the loved one — such as this rather quaint verse:

> *Good morning to you Valentine,*
> *Curl you locks as I do mine,*
> *One before and two behind,*
> *Good morning to you Valentine.*

The habit of giving greetings and presents to friends on special feast days is also timeless. The ancient Egyptians exchanged perfume and inscribed scarabs as tokens of good will. The

Romans gave olive or laurel branches often coated with gold leaf. In Saxon England and after on St Valentine's day it was customary for a boy to give the girl of his choice a love token, usually a pair of gloves. The glove was a sign of authority in olden times, and this may have had added significance.

In Norwich years ago it was the general custom to give presents on St Valentine's eve and this still survives to a certain extent. Packages containing all manner of gifts were laid on doorsteps all over the city. They were anonymous, and usually just bore the message — 'Good-morrow to you Valentine'. It was normal practice to ring or knock on the door, after depositing the package, and then disappear. Some parcels contained valuable presents while others were given as a kind of joke, being wrapped in many layers of paper punctuated at intervals by little notes of encouragement such as — 'Never despair' or 'The brightest jewel is in the deepest mine' or 'Happy is he that expecteth nothing'. The final present was probably a wooden spoon or some such trivial item.

In 1872 the Post Office declared that parcels not exceeding 12 ounces in weight could be sent by letter post. This news meant that in Norwich alone two days before St Valentine's eve 150,000 letters containing small gifts were sent through the post. From that time onwards the custom of leaving presents on doorsteps dwindled. Nevertheless, the tradition of giving Valentine presents in Norwich developed into a thriving business. Thousands of pounds were spent on gifts for the office, domestic and personal use. Local papers advertised, wall placards advertised and the town criers too advertised by ringing bells and shouting the advantages of buying gifts at certain local stores. The presents sent in a secret manner included oranges, work boxes, squeaking dolls, silver pencils and holders, books and various trinkets. One person found a library chair deposited on her door step!

In other parts of the country presents were also distributed — mainly for children, and included cakes, apples and coins. In Peterborough, sweet plum buns were made and eaten called Valentine buns, and in Uppingham, gingerbread was given to lovers. In Rutland, buns were made and are still being made for children on this day. They are lozenge shaped sponge cakes, shaped like a weaver's shuttle, and called 'Plum Shuttles'.

Weaving and lace making were cottage industries in the past in that part of the world.

The aristocracy enjoyed the Valentine custom in perhaps a more sophisticated and decidedly more costly way. It is reported that in the seventeenth century it was quite normal for respectable married couples to draw for Valentines and the pairing lasted until the next Valentine day. Some men were thankful that they drew children and not adult females for their Valentines as they were not expected to give such costly presents to a child! Most ladies of fashion expected expensive gifts such as silk stockings, garters, jewelry and perfume from their Valentines. Samuel Pepys in his diary in 1667 recorded that a certain Mrs. Stewart was the Duke of York's Valentine and that he gave her a jewel worth at least £800, and the following year the same lady was Lord Mandeville's Valentine and he gave her a ring worth about £300. She must have been quite an attractive lady!

The Valentine Card
Parchment was scarce, and as the majority of people were illiterate it was not until the fifteenth century that the first greeting card was produced. Master wood engravers instigated this custom. The forerunner of the paper Valentine was first seen in the seventeenth century and the first printed Valentine may have been the frontispiece of *A Valentine Writer*, a book of verses published in 1669 that were designed to help the inarticulate and mentally handicapped. By 1800 hand printed copperplates by such artists as Francesco Bartolozzi were much in demand by the upper classes. Woodcuts and lithographs quarto size, some with embossed frames were also popular.

With the introduction of the penny postage and the use of envelopes in 1840 the popularity of the Valentine card increased, as indeed did all forms of correspondence. The Valentine card took on a much more delicate form in Victorian times. It was often made out of lace paper, velvet, and satin ribbons, embossed with the best quality material. These cards often had trick or secret panels in them, hiding secret messages to the girls concerned. This was because Victorian fathers were very strict and would not allow their daughters to receive any sort of correspondence unless they had first read it and decided whether or not it was suitable! Messages were therefore often hidden under folds of lace or ribbons. Later the traditional card printed its love messages in the form of a verse similar to those repeated by people centuries before.

The censorship of strict Victorian fathers and the element of mystery and surprise experienced by those who in former times played the lottery pairing game has undoubtedly contributed to the reason why Valentine cards are, by tradition, anonymous.

The custom of sending Valentine cards almost came to an end in the early part of the present century. However, in the thirties it was revived, and now like many other festivals has been highly commercialised. In America for instance, more greeting cards are sent than in any other country — and they become more elaborate and expensive every year. But nothing can replace in value the first, hand engraved and painted Valentine cards. They are collector's items and are worth a fortune.

ST VALENTINE'S DAY CUSTOMS

Valentine Buns are relatively easy to make and would be particularly popular at a children's party.

Ingredients:

1½ lbs (600 g) plain flour
4 ozs (100 g) castor sugar
2 ozs (50 g) chopped peel
½ pint (250 ml) milk and
½ pint (250 ml) of water to
  mix

4 ozs (100 g) butter
4 ozs (100 g) clean currants
1 oz (25 g) yeast

Method: Crumble yeast with a teaspoonful of sugar until it liquifies. Warm a large mixing bowl, sift flour, and rub in fat. Add sugar, currants and peel and mix well. Add yeast to mixture and water and milk to make a soft dough. Leave to prove for about 30 minutes. Turn out dough onto a lightly floured board and kneed until smooth. Pull into pieces and shape like small sausages or ovals, pointed at both ends, similar to a weaver's shuttle. Arrange on a warm baking tray and leave for another 20 minutes. Then bake in a pre-heated oven — 375° F or gas 5 for about 15 to 20 minutes, or until golden brown. These buns are delicious if eaten hot with butter at teatime.

Children like making *Valentine Cards* and here are the instructions for making one:

You will need:

a small silver covered cardboard cake stand approximately eight inches (20 cms) in diameter

one paper doyley roughly ten inches (25 cms) in diameter and another doyley approximately three inches (seven and a half cms)

a piece of cardboard cut to the same size as the silver piece

a yard or metre of coloured ribbon — red is a good colour

a sheet of red or white paper, glue, paper clip, crayons or paints

Glue the large doyley with a spot of glue here and there and all round the edges to the back of the silver round of cardboard, so that the edges show all round like a lace frill. Draw a heart shape on the red paper, or on the white paper and colour it red, cut this out and stick it onto the front of the silver disc. Draw an arrow through the heart and write above it, 'To my Valentine'. Decorate the other piece of card as you will, with lover's knots or red hearts round the edge. In the centre print a Valentine verse and glue the small doyley at one spot so that it can be lifted to show the verse underneath. Cut a piece approximately four inches (10 cms) off the ribbon, glue it and place it over the two pieces of cardboard on the left side so joining the two pieces of card together with the silver piece on top. Tie the rest of the ribbon into a bow, cutting off any that is too long. Using the push through paper clip fix the bow in the centre of the ribbon hinge.

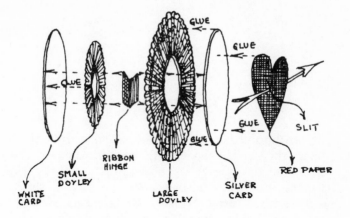

GLUE

GLUE

GLUE

GLUE

SLIT

RED PAPER

SILVER
CARD

LARGE
DOYLEY

RIBBON
HINGE

SMALL
DOYLEY

WHITE
CARD

TO MY VALENTINE

Valentine card.

SHROVETIDE

Long ago Shrovetide played an important part in the lives of ordinary people. The worst of the winter was over, and while people waited eagerly for warmer days, they thankfully welcomed Shrovetide and all it stood for. The word shrove is the past tense of the verb to shrive — which means to confess sins. People were called to church on Shrove Tuesday to be shrived — that is to be forgiven and cleansed of all sins before the coming of Lent, which began on the following day — Ash Wednesday.

Most people, however, regarded this event as a holiday for feasting and merrymaking — the last chance for enjoyment before the six long, dour weeks of the Lenten fast. Shrovetide lasted for four days in former times, beginning on Shrove Saturday, over Shrove Sunday or Quinquagesima, Collop Monday and ending on Shrove Tuesday or Pancake Day. The reason for such feasting was that during Lent people were forbidden to eat eggs, butter and other fats, meat and all rich food in general. These ingredients had to be cooked and eaten on the feast days of Shrovetide, leaving larders empty of all but the bare necessities.

European countries have either a Butter or Cheese week preceding Lent, or they honour Pancake Day as we do. Italy has Pretzels which are now eaten all over the world, and in Sweden Semlors are very popular, being rich buns filled with almond paste. In Belgium and Holland pancakes are made in the same way as in Britain. The Shrovetide tradition in Denmark long ago was for children to wake their parents with decorated birch rods, singing their demand for buns, which are similar to the Hot Cross Buns eaten on Good Friday. An old custom in that country of 'tilting the barrel' was practised by children — the idea being to smash a barrel with sticks, to let out an imaginary cat, but when the barrel was finally opened, it was found to contain sweets and oranges — which were not imaginary!

Shrove Saturday in Oxfordshire was called Egg Feast Day or

Egg Saturday. A popular name for Egg Saturday was 'Brusting Saturday'. Eggs were often limed or pickled to preserve them during the winter months, and a gift of a pickled egg was a gift indeed to a hungry child.

Shrove Sunday was another feast and rest day. People often sat and talked and planned the revelries and games which were to take place on the following two days. In St Ives in Cornwall, for instance, an annual hurling match was prepared for Collop Monday to be played on the sands. Two goal posts were erected and the game was played in the space between. A ball about the size of a cricket ball was used, usually made of cork or light wood, and sometimes covered with silver. All the Toms, Wills, and Johns played on one side and those with other names on the other.

Collop Monday, the day before Pancake Day was so called because people especially in the North of England, cooked and ate collops on this day. Collops were in fact our well known dish of bacon and eggs, and this may be where the tradition sprang from. The word collop is derived from the Norse, meaning a slice of meat, and probably entered our language during Saxon times when Norsemen were constantly invading our shores. Children often gave their teachers gifts of collops on Collop Monday.

The old way to cook eggs and bacon is given in a recipe dated 1615 in a book called *The English Hus-wife* by Gervase Markham, and reads like this — 'To have the best collops and eggs you shall take the bacon, cutting away the rind, cut the collops into thin slices, lay them on a dish and put hot water on them, so let it stand for an howere or two. Then drain away the water clean, and pat them dry, and ley them one by one on a dish and set before the fire so they may toast, and turn them so they may toast throwe and throwe, which when done, take your eggs and breake into a dish and put a spoonful of vinegar with them and set with water on the fire and let them take a boyle or two, and then take up and trim, and drie them, dishing up the collops lay the eggs upon them, and this way is the best way and most wholesome.'

Another story which explains the custom of making pancakes at Shrovetide dates from Saxon times: It appears that when the village settlement at Linby in Yorkshire was over-run by invading Danes, the men fled to the forest leaving their women and children to cope with their new Danish masters. The women did not appreciate this arrangement, and after a secret meeting conspired to massacre the Danes on Ash Wednesday. A kitchen knife was to be the murder weapon. It was essential that every woman agreed to the plan, and all promised to make pancakes the day before Ash Wednesday as a pledge to carry out her part in the conspiracy. And so in every Saxon hut, the day before the beginning of Lent there was a delicious smell of cooking pancakes. The Danes were too tired and hungry to notice anything amiss, and gladly ate what was put before them — golden pancakes sweetened and flavoured with honey and berry juices. Soon the invaders were asleep, stretched out on soft furs in corners of Saxon homes. Then the women bravely waited until the early hours of Ash Wednesday morning before stabbing their unwelcome visitors with sharp kitchen knives. When all the Danes had been killed the women joyfully ran out and called their menfolk back home. When the men heard what had happened they were filled with admiration for their wives. According to legend, the wives then made another batch of pancakes for the hungry men, and these pancakes were enjoyed as never before. Every year after that pancakes were made on the day before Ash Wednesday, to celebrate the victory over the Danes, and the idea spread to other parts of the country — and so Pancake Day came into being.

In Taylor's *Jack-a-Lent* written in 1630 he puts forward this recipe entitled 'Seventeenth Century Pancakes'.

'There is a thing called wheaten flowre, which the cookes doe mingle with water, egges, spice and other tragicall, magicall inchantments, and they put it by little into a frying pan of boyling suet where it makes a confused dismall hissing (like the Learnean snakes in the reeds of Acheron, Stix, or Phlegeton), untill, at last by the skills of the Cooke, it is transformed into the forme of a Flap-jack, cal'd a Pancake, which ominous incantation the ignaorant people doe devoure very greedily'.

Polydore Virgil affirms that the season of Shrovetide sprung from the Roman pre-Christian feasts of Bacchus, god of wine and life, and patron of poets. When Christianity was accepted, the last feast day before Lent was merged with the Bacchus festival to form Pancake Day as we know it.

The pupils of Eton School, until the nineteenth century wrote poems at Shrovetide in honour of Bacchus, and the verses composed by the boys of the sixth and seventh forms were displayed in the school, pinned on the inside doors.

Another curious custom which is still practised on Shrove Tuesday is the Pancake Greaze at Westminster School. No one knows how it started but the first written tract referring to the ritual appeared in the early part of the eighteenth century.

Years ago the scholars of Westminster School were hardy, tough and rough individuals who fought for everything they thought necessary, including their food, I suspect. In those days the masters took their meals with scholars and the Shrovetide custom may have been started by a Dean suggesting that a pancake be thrown amongst the boys on Pancake Day, and that the one who could retrieve it whole should be given a golden guinea. The annual ritual of the cook bringing the pancake into the one long high room with its hammer roof, where the whole school was taught, must have created an unforgettable scene when more than 300 boys took part. The cook tossed the pancake over the high bar which divided the junior and upper forms, and you can be sure that there must have been many casualties as a result of the scrimmage. The masters must have enjoyed the robust entertainment and probably wagered bets on possible winners!

According to Charles Keeley, one time archivist at Westminster School, the number of boys taking part in this century has been reduced for practical purposes. In modern times only the representatives of each form are contestants, and the senior boys need not take part at all, if they do not wish. The boy with the largest piece of pancake is awarded the guinea, which he accepts but later exchanges it with the Dean for its equivalent value. The pancake is specially prepared with horse hair, true to tradition, but the whole ceremony is carried out in a benign good humoured atmosphere which is in complete contrast to the scenes of long ago. The Dean then 'begs a play' — that is to say, asks for a holiday before leaving, and the reaction to this at least has not changed! The ritual still takes place in the old school-room and the pancake is still thrown over the same bar, as has been the custom for centuries.

Another old school custom practised on Pancake Day was the process of 'barring out'. Pupils and masters alike waited for the toll of the Pancake bell, and when it was heard the boys enticed the master outside the school, and then locked themselves in saying that they would not let the master in until he declared a holiday. This was just a ritual and the master willingly agreed, and all went off to enjoy the day as they pleased.

A favourite occupation of children from poor families on this special day, was to go from door to door, asking for contributions for Shrovetide. Eggs, flour, bacon or money were usually requested. The 'well to do houses' with the 'best pictures' — that is those with large sides of bacon hanging in the kitchens, were the ones which were most favoured.

The Pancake Bell
The Pancake bell was heard in most parishes on Shrove Tuesday until the nineteenth and early twentieth centuries. It was usually rung in the morning, and told the villagers three things. Firstly, time for shriving at the church, secondly, time to start a holiday by downing tools and closing shops and thirdly, time to start making pancakes.

In many places the people themselves were allowed to ring the bells on Pancake Day. Anyone who wished to do this was allowed to climb into the belfry and 'have a go'. At All Saints, Maidstone, the bell was called the Fritter-bell. In Daventry, Northampton-shire the bell was called Pan-burn, and in Wellingborough the mellow toned sixth bell was called Old Pancake and weighed about 16 cwt. Tradition has it that while Old Pancake was ringing pancakes were thrown out of the tower windows.

In Hoddesdon, Hertfordshire, the Curfew bell was rung at four a.m. to allow pancake making to begin, and was rung again at eight p.m. to tell people to stop making pancakes and put fires out, for safety. It is interesting to note that a half bell shaped instrument was then put over the dying embers of the fire, to ensure that the fire was put out in accordance with the Curfew bell, and that this piece of equipment was called a couvre feu or curfew.

In Cheshire the pancake bell was called the Guttit bell, and no explanation is needed for this, I think! There is a tragic story connected with Wilmslow church, Cheshire. About 200 years ago a boy aged about ten climbed into the belfry to look at the bells. The bell ringers below had no notion that he was there and soon the heavy bells swept the poor child round and round. The ringers did not hear his cries, and it was not until his blood fell on them, did they realise what had happened.

Another story about bell ringing concerns York minster. As elsewhere, public ringing was allowed and, in fact, here they also had the 'run of the church' on this day. The local people had a habit of singing in the church, and not hymns, either! The old proverb refers to this:

> *When Pancake bell begins to ring,*
> *All Halifax lads begin to sing.*

When a certain Dr Lake was made an official of York minster, in about 1670, he was determined to put a stop to public bell ringing and other customs which he thought desicrated the church. Dr Lake was a brave man and risked his life when ordering the rabble out of the church on Shrove Tuesday. The story goes that he went into the crowd and plucked the hats off some of their heads. It was a miracle that he was not attacked and killed as the locals were incensed at this attack on their pleasures and privileges which they and their ancestors had enjoyed since ancient times. However, Dr Lake at last succeeded in terminating these 'vulgar' practices, before he moved away from Yorkshire to take up other church work. Later he was made a bishop and was one of the seven bishops who were committed to the Tower of London by James II, 1688, because he failed to support the king over certain religious matters. He died in 1689, but remained true to the Church of England until his death.

Pancake Competitions

Probably the most interesting place on Shrove Tuesday in Britain today is the town of Olney in Buckinghamshire. For it is here that the famous annual pancake race is run. Tradition holds that the race was first started in the fifteenth century, although there is no early written reference to this. The story goes that when the pancake bell was rung on Shrove Tuesday, a harrassed housewife ran to the church still clutching her pancake skillet — so afraid was she at being late for the shriving service. Or another idea was that housewives bribed the bell ringers with pancakes to ring the bell early in the day and so lengthen the holiday time. In 1923 Thomas Wright wrote a poem of 56 verses entitled 'The

Pancake Bell' — telling of a race run in Olney in the reign of Good Queen Bess. The first verse goes like this:

> *At Olney when good Bess was queen,*
> *The pancake bell was rung,*
> *And sweeter sound ne'er scurried*
> *From steeple, crowde or tongue.*

The custom was not kept up during the last war, but was revived by the Reverend Collins, vicar of Olney, in 1947, and the idea was accepted with enthusiasm. Since then the pancake race at Olney has created interest all over the world and has emerged as a major social event for the town.

The day is proclaimed a holiday, and before the race contestants are vetted to ensure that they have resided in the towns of Olney or Warrington for at least three months. Those taking part must be suitably dressed for the occasion, wearing pinafores and headscarves. The pancakes must be tossed under starter's orders, and again after passing the finishing line, before the winner is announced. The successful candidate receives the Kiss of Peace from the vicar with the words — 'The Peace of the Lord be always with you'. The contestants then attend the shriving service in the Olney parish church which is always packed on this occasion. In the evening there is often a special pancake party held in the village hall, to which everyone is invited.

In 1949 a picture and an account of the Olney race appeared in a local newspaper in Liberal, U.S.A. This event attracted the attention of some civic organisers namely the Jaycees and they decided it might be fun to organise a similar pancake race for the women of Liberal — actually racing the housewives of Olney for the fastest time, on a similar course. After some persuading some of the housewives of Liberal agreed to take part and the event became as popular as it is in Olney. The course is 415 yards (379m) long and is shaped like an S. The housewives of Olney run over cobble and tarmac streets, and the Americans over asphalt and brick surfaces. The vicar of Olney has visited Liberal to witness the pancake celebrations and visitors from Liberal have been entertained in Olney in the same manner.

The pancake festival in Liberal lasts for three or four days — true to old Shrovetide tradition. On the preceding Sunday there is a dedication service. On Monday a Miss Flipper beauty contest, and Tuesday is claimed as a holiday and begins with a pancake breakfast in the armoury. There are races for children of all ages, and at 11.55 a.m. the big race is run. As in Olney the winner receives the Kiss of Peace administered by the British Consul. She also receives a prayer book and a silver tray. The winning town holding the fastest time is presented with a travelling trophy — a pancake griddle engraved with the names of past winners.

Also in Liberal there are pancake eating competitions, parades and bands. In 1975 a huge pancake was made measuring 2 inches (five cm) by 12 feet (three and a half m) across, and was baked to set a new record for the Guinness Book of Records.

On one of his visits to Liberal the vicar of Olney presented the town with a recording of the peal of Olney church bells as played on Pancake Day. This recording has been played in Liberal at the beginning of the big race ever since.

Many other places in Britain now have pancake races on Shrove Tuesday. In Norwich for instance, an annual pancake race is run in Chapelfield, a park in the centre of the city.

Not only were there pancake races long ago, but also pancake eating competitions. Many poor people near to starvation were only to pleased to join in — and the quantity of pancakes eaten was enormous. A youth at Cheltenham College by the name of Hughes, over a hundred years ago, was credited with having eaten 36 pancakes and was the admiration of all. He was of course proclaimed the winner of that particular competition. It was reported that he was long, lean and hungry looking — probably suffering from worms — and that by the end of the week he was just as hungry as ever!

There are many fortune customs connected with the making of pancakes — one being that the maid who could successfully cook and toss a pancake on Shrove Tuesday would be married within the year. If an unfortunate pancake maker accidentally tossed her pancakes on the fire, then tradition has it that she was carried outside and deposited on the nearest dunghill!

It has always been regarded as a lucky omen to make pancakes over Shrovetide, and a saying from Yorkshire tells us — 'Eat pancakes on Shrove Tuesday and grey peas on Ash Wednesday, and you will have money in your pocket all the year round.'

Sports and Games

Apart from pancake eating — the main pastime on Shrove Tuesday was the playing of games, in which it seems all the community who were able took part! The most popular and widespread game throughout Britain was football — but it was far different from the game we know today. The idea was probably first introduced by the Romans when they invaded Britain. The game was called 'Camping' for many years in the South of England, and the reason for this is obscure. The 'pitch' had no set boundaries but usually stretched for miles through villages, towns and countryside. Sometimes hundreds of players took part in the game which could last all day.

In Derbyshire, for instance, the parishioners of All Saints with their goal at Nun's Mill played their rivals the parishioners from St Peter's and their goal was Gallows Balk. The contestants stood at opposite sides of the market place at noon, a large football was then tossed in the centre — and thus the game began. The object of St Peter's was to get the ball into Derwent river via Mortledge Brook, and All Saint's aim was to kick the ball westwards as far as possible. It is reported that people taking part numbered more than a thousand and because of this shops closed and shop keepers boarded up their windows, as indeed did the inhabitants of many private dwellings.

At Workington, Cumberland, the Uppies or colliers played the Downies or sailors in the town. The game was played for long hours and knew no boundaries, and many thousands of spectators cheered the numerous players.

At Dorking the game of Camping boasted of a very ancient past. The ritual started off on Shrove Tuesday with a fancy dress parade led by a man carrying three footballs on a triangular frame over which was the motto: 'Kick away, both Whig and Tory, Wind and Water, Dorking's Glory'.

It is not known why the football was referred to as 'Wind and Water', but some historians think that the 'wind' may refer to the inflation of the ball and the 'water' to the ducking that the contestants gave each other in a nearby brook during the course of the game! The game was stopped at six o'clock and the players then gathered round the ball as it lay on the ground, and gave a hearty hurrah, which meant that the pastime was over for another year.

Some sports played over Shrovetide involved animals and were very cruel. Dog and bear baiting were common, as was cock fighting which was usually held in the school yard. As Shrove Tuesday was a public holiday, villagers gathered and gambled alongside pupils and masters — and the cocks were often kept for weeks on the school premises before the event.

Another vicious sport usually practised at fairs and markets was the game of 'throwing at cocks'. Cocks were tethered to stakes and competitors paid money to throw sticks and stones at them at 25 paces — usually 2d for six throws. If the bird was stunned and did not recover before the thrower could pick it up then it became his property. The origin of cock throwing is obscure, but an old story tells us that the untimely crowing of a cock frustrated well laid plans by the English to massacre a Danish settlement on our shores. Cocks were punished for centuries on Shrove Tuesday as a result. A legacy of cock throwing is preserved in the popular game of bowls, where the aim of the players is to hit the 'cock' — a small white ball. All cruel sports of this kind were gradually phased out and made illegal during the nineteenth century.

It is possible that the beginnings of a popular game sprang from this ill-treatment of cocks on Pancake Day. There must have been plenty of feathers available and it did not take long for some enterprising person to find a use for them. Stuck into a cork, or perhaps an old weaving shuttle, the first shuttlecock came into use, and was soon being hit back and forth by players using pieces of wood as bats. The game was first called Battledore and Shuttlecock or Shuttlefeather, and was widely played in the weaving counties of Leicestershire and Yorkshire over Shrovetide. A Battledore has been described as a wooden instrument shaped like a canoe paddle used to beat the washing in olden times. Probably the first Battledores were in reality washing beaters! The word has a Spanish derivation — batidor which means beater.

The word shuttle is derived from the Anglo-Saxon — sceotan — which means to shoot. As the shuttle on the weaving loom carrying the weft thread was shot to and fro across the warp threads, so the shuttlecock was hit to and fro by players using Battledores — this is probably how it got its name.

In any case the game was played in the streets most enthusiastically in many northern towns, and of course this is how the game of Badminton originated. Children often chanted this old couplet while playing this game.

> *Shuttlecock, shuttlecock, tell me true,*
> *How many years have I to go through?*
> *One, two, three, four, five — (etc.)*

Badminton was first played as an organised game at Badminton House, on the Duke of Beaufort's estate, in Gloucestershire. Apparently the first games were played with toy Battledores — toy bats with strings of parchment stretched across them, and shuttlecocks, in a room which had a string stretched across the centre. There was no net in the beginning which was around 1865. Several years later an authorised game with recognised rules developed. The game was also played in India early on, the idea being introduced by British rulers.

After the winter months, the coming of Shrovetide seemed to be the signal for the commencement of many open air games. Skipping, tug o' war, marbles and top whipping were very popular, and some of these games and their histories have been dealt with in the Eastertide section.

A game called 'Prison Bars' was played with great zeal in Chester and other northern towns — often between rival villages or pubs. The teams usually consisted of ten to twelve men with a base at each end of the playing area. The game commenced with a kind of hand linked tug o' war, and when one member broke the link, then a member of the opposite team chased him in the 'field'. He was immediately chased in his turn by one of the opposing side and so on until all the players were chasing each other. When one was touched by the opposition before reaching his base then he became a member of the rival side, and the whole process started again. The winning team was of course the one with most players at the end of the game. The winners were then given gay ribbons and streamers which they proudly wore round their hats, for the rest of the day. This game as far as I know is not played today, but I am sure it would provide a lot of fun if it was revived — and it does not require any special equipment.

Horse racing at Chester owes its beginnings to old Pancake Day customs. On this holiday the townspeople gathered on the Roodee, which is a piece of common land flanked by the river Dee just outside the city. All sorts of games were played and many different guilds came with various offerings. The Shoemakers' guild brought a football costing not less than 3s 4d (17p) — and a wild game of football was played. Those who had been married during the past year paid homage by a gift to the Drapers' Company, and this was changed to a silver arrow and used as a prize for which the town archers competed. The Sadlers gave a ball of silk which was thrown to the crowd. So many people were hurt while scrambling for it, that in 1540 the mayor, one Henry Gee, ordered a silver bell to be substituted instead, and that a horse race should be run to determine who should receive the bell. This was the origin of the Chester races. In 1623 the prize was increased — and one silver cup to the value of £8.00 was offered.

The name Roodee originates from Roodeye, Eye of the Cross (in Latin, Oculus Crucis) or alternatively Island of the Cross — rood — cross, eye — island). There is a legend that a cross fell in the river at Hawarden and floated upsteam to Chester. The Chester races at still run on the Roodee today, and are normally held three times a year — in May, July and September.

A game played by children in Kent and other southern counties on Shrove Tuesday has long been forgotten, and in fact it has been stated that it was so old that it may have originated with the first pagan rituals ever practised; this was called Holly Boy and Ivy Girl. The Ivy Girl was often made at harvest time like a corn dolly out of strands of corn, and decorated with ivy. It was then kept through the winter as a good luck symbol representing the continuance of life — ivy was used because it is an evergreen.

Holly has been regarded as having magical and healing powers from pagan times, although it is not known when the Holly Boy came into being. But it was the custom on Shrove Tuesday many centuries ago for the boys to make a figure similar to the Ivy Girl, and decorated with holly. When the figures were completed the girls carried their Ivy Girl to one part of the village, and the boys carried their Holly Boy to another part. The object of the game was to raid the camp of the opposite sex and carry off the effigy, and burn it on a bonfire amongst much hilarity and amusement.

SHROVETIDE CUSTOMS

Shrovetide is celebrated in Europe and also in other parts of the world. Many countries have their own special dishes, and nearer home recipes vary according to the locality.

In Ireland buttermilk pancakes are made and the ingredients include buttermilk, syrup and flour. In Scotland many traditional dishes are cooked at Shrovetide. An oatmeal pancake called a Sauty Bannock is very popular and is made out of fine oatmeal soaked in broth with eggs whisked into the mixture — and cooked in the normal way.

In England, too, although we usually keep to the traditional pancake recipe, many other districts in the past have made differing dishes. For a start here is the basic pancake recipe:

½ lb (220 g) self raising flour	1½ oz (40 g) lard
1 pint (500 ml) milk	1 lemon
2 eggs	sugar for sprinkling
pinch of salt	

Sieve the flour and salt into a basin, making a well in the centre. Break the eggs one at a time and pour into the well. Gradually beat the eggs and flour together, adding milk little by little until a creamy consistency has been reached. Beat the batter for a few minutes to aerate it, and leave to stand for an hour or so if possible.

Heat a frying pan or griddle with a little lard and pour enough batter to cover the area needed. Cook until the top is dry, and then either toss or turn the pancake and cook the other side until brown.

Turn out onto greaseproof paper, sprinkle with sugar and lemon juice as desired and roll up before serving.

Nowadays pancakes are sometimes made with a handful of dried fruit such as currants or sultanas added to the mixture before cooking, and then served up with ice-cream. But personally I prefer the old way of flavouring with sugar and lemon juice.

In Baldock, Hertfordshire, Pancake Day was called Doughnut Day, and of course doughnuts were made and eaten instead of pancakes. The idea may have filtered through in some way from Austria where doughnuts are very popular. Although the people of Baldock have forgotten this custom, I managed to trace a recipe for Baldock doughnuts as sent in to 'The Farmer's Weekly' by Margaret Coleman. Here it is:

1 large cupful granulated sugar	a good sprinkling of currants
1 large cupful milk	1½ teaspoons of cream of tartar
2 oz (50 g) butter	¼ teaspoon bicarbonate of soda
2 small eggs	a little flour

Mix all the dry ingredients well and add the milk and beaten eggs and enough flour to make a workable paste. Roll into small balls (they will double their size) and fry in deep fat till a nice nut-brown. Toss in sugar and serve immediately. This quantity of ingredients will make a substantial number!'

In Norwich Coquille buns were made and eaten over Shrovetide many years ago. The origin of the name presents a mystery which has not been solved. Coquille is a French word meaning shell or shell-shaped. I made various inquiries as to the origin of the custom and was very gratified by the response. A letter in the local paper brought in ideas, information and recipes, and it was clear that this old Norfolk custom has not been forgotten. The buns were known as Coquilles, Cocheals or Cook-eels, and it has been suggested that the American term 'cookie' stemmed from this source. Coquille buns were made and sold by Norwich bakers and were even sold in the streets many years ago. Here is an old street cry which bears witness to this:

> *Hot penny co-quill-es,*
> *Smoking all hot,*
> *Smoking all hot,*
> *Hot penny co-quill-es.*

A lady wrote to me and suggested that perhaps the word coquille was taken from the Coquille St Jacques badges which were awarded in the Middle Ages to pilgrims who had made the pilgrimage to the Spanish shrine of Santiago de Compostela. The badges were shell-shaped and Coquille buns may have been made shell-shaped in former days to commemorate the awards.

Today Coquille St Jacques is a dish of sea food served up on a large scallop shell.

Norwich people still make Coquille buns over Shrovetide, and one Norwich baker at least still sells them in his shop on Pancake Day.

Some recipes for Coquille buns include yeast but here is a simple basic recipe which you might like to try:

1 lb (500 g) self raising flour	2 teaspoons mixed spice
2 oz (50 g) lard	2 tablespoons mixed cake fruit
2 oz (50 g) margarine	1 egg, and a little milk
½ breakfast cup sugar	

Rub lard and margarine into flour with the fingers. Mix in sugar, spice and fruit. Beat egg and add with enough milk to make a soft dough. Roll out two inches (five cms) thick on a floured board and cut into squares. Cook in a moderate oven 375°F or Gas Mark 5, for about 20 minutes or until golden brown. Serve split and buttered.

If extra spicy buns are preferred, grated nutmeg and cinnamon can be added.

Things For Children To Do

Pancake Day provides many opportunities for children to do things for themselves without much help from adults. They could hold a pancake party giving their friends eggs and bacon (collops), pancakes, doughnuts, Coquille buns and other food linked with Shrovetide. Pancake tossing competitions could be held and chef hats and aprons made out of a roll of cheap white wallpaper lining.

For a *chef hat* a piece of white paper measuring roughly 36x10 inches (90x25 cms) and a large square or circle of white tissue paper for the top, paste or glue is all that is needed. The children should roll the large piece of white paper into a tube to fit their heads and then stick the edges down with glue. The tissue paper can be puffed out and the top of the tube dabbed inside with glue — then the edges of the tissue paper pushed into the top of the tube and stuck down. If the tissue paper is then puffed out over the tube it makes the shape of a chef's hat. *Waist aprons* can be made out of a piece of white paper measuring approx 12x18 inches (30x45cms) and a long piece of white tape approximately five feet (one and a half metres) long can be stuck onto the top of the paper on the 12 inches (30 cms) side, so that equal lengths of the tape are left each side for tying.

Another competition might involve making *Ivy Girls* and *Holly Boys* using old rag figures and decorated with holly and ivy. A method of making rag dolls is described in the Guy Fawkes section. The ivy dolls would be quite easy to make using trails of ivy for skirt decoration and hair. Holly dolls may be more difficult for obvious reasons and gloves would have to be worn while doing this. Pieces of holly could be pinned or stitched onto clothing already covering the doll. Holly leaves could be used for hair, separate leaves glued to the head would look very effective. There might be a prize for the best doll but in any case the children would have the satisfaction of making something original. It would be open to question whether or not the children would then want to play the rest of the game as children did long ago and burn the dolls on bonfires afterwards!

Some of the Shrovetide *games* could be revived. Prison Bars for instance might be popular as well as spinning the top, marbles and skipping not forgetting the tug 'o war. Simple badminton played outside could provide a lot of fun. A net might be made out of an old piece of curtain netting approximately 10x2 feet (3mx60cms), with a piece of string threaded through the top about 20 feet (6m) long — or long enough to tie each end round a convenient post or tree. Second hand rackets can be bought cheaply and plastic shuttles are durable and only cost a few pence.

The children might hold a Pancake Fair and sell the produce to raise money for various charities. Children could be encouraged to write their own pancake poems and stories as the pupils of Eton did in honour of Bacchus the patron saint of poets. They might even like to bring out their own Pancake Day magazine and include all news of Shrovetide happenings in their locality.

MOTHERING SUNDAY

The fourth Sunday in Lent called Mid Lent Sunday or Mothering Sunday, provided a welcome break from the strict fasting that people followed centuries ago. The origin of Mothering Sunday is obscure and one explanation is that it must have been about the time when Jesus was conceived — nine months before Christmas Day, his birthday. But most historians seem to agree that the origin stemmed from the tradition of parishioners worshipping at the Mother Church in their district — perhaps the cathedral or large parish church. On this day they left their village chapels and walked many miles to attend the Mothering Day service, bringing offerings and thanks to the Mother Church. One can imagine that in the days of no transport it must have been a very special occasion for people of long ago. From this sprang the idea of Mothering Sunday as a day to honour the mother of the family — a tradition that has not wavered throughout the years. Young people working away from home were given the day off to visit their mother and take her presents of trinkets, fancy linen, tea, money or more usually a cake called a simnel and a posy of wild flowers picked on the way to the church.

After the family service at the Mother Church, the united family went home to enjoy a dinner of roast lamb or veal often followed by rice pudding, fig pie or plum pudding. It was washed down with mulled ale — a mixture of ale, sugar and spices, or frumenty. The latter was a drink enjoyed by children mostly, made up of wheat grains boiled in milk with sugar and spices added.

In some places fig pies were very popular especially in the north of England. They consisted of dried figs, treacle, sugar and spices, cooked in a pastry case. Sometimes Mothering Sunday was called Fig Pie Sunday or Mulled Ale Sunday.

Young girls often brought their boyfriends to be introduced to their mothers on Mothering Sunday. Sometimes it was the boy who brought the cake for his future mother-in-law, and recited this verse to his sweetheart before the journey:

> *And I'll to thee a simnel bring*
> *'Gainst thou goest a-mothering;*
> *So that when she blesses thee,*
> *Half the blessing thou'st give*
> *me.*

There are various explanations about the origin of the simnel cake but it is agreed by most people that the name simnel is derived from a Latin word 'similia' meaning fine wheat flour. One story links the name with Lambert Simnel, the pretender to the throne in the reign of Henry VII. It has been said that his father was a baker and not a joiner as is commonly held, and that the elder Simnel made these special cakes to commemorate the plan of his son and his friends to gain the throne.

Another story which comes from the west of England tells us that a couple from Shrewsbury could not agree whether to boil or bake a special cake that they wished to make, so they compromised by both boiling and baking it. The man's name was Simon and his wife's name was Nell!

But we know that simnel cakes were being made before the Norman Conquest. In 1042, it states in the Annuals of Winchester that King Edward ordered simnels numbering a hundred to be sent to convents of Winchester, Worcester and Westminster as presents whenever he or future kings of England stayed there.

Simnel cakes have been made in various places throughout Britain from time immemorial. The most famous of these are Shrewsbury, Devizes and Bury. It is interesting to read how different the recipes are. The Shrewsbury simnel has a thick crust of saffron bread enclosing the rest of the ingredients. The Devizes simnel has no bread crust but the ingredients are kneaded into a paste and the cake shaped and cooked like a star. The Bury simnel is usually a fairly flat cake with the thickest part in the centre and turned up at the edges. The recipe for the Bury simnel was kept a closely guarded secret by a family of pastry cooks for generations. The 'trade secret' has now leaked out — and here are the ingredients needed for the cake:

flour 2½ lbs (1 kg 220 g)
butter ½ lb (220 g)
lard ½ lb (220 g)
sugar 1½ lb (220 g)
salts of ammonia 1 oz (25 g)
almonds ¾ lb (350 g)
a few bitter almonds if desired

currants 4 lbs (2 kg)
nutmeg ½ oz (12 g)
candied peel ½ lb (220 g)
cinnamon ½ oz (12 g)
5 eggs
a little milk is necessary

Method. Rub the butter and lard into the floor. Pound the salts of ammonia and mix well. Then, mix in well all the other dry ingredients. Blend them with the eggs which should be made into the form of a batch loaf about 18 inches (45 cms) and more across, two and a half to three inches (five to seven and a half centimetres) and round in shape. Bake in a slow oven for one and a half to two hours.

This recipe can be found in *Good Things in England* by Florence White and I have added metric equivalents.

Most of the simnel cakes made and sold in this century have been of the Shrewsbury type — and I myself have always thought of a simnel being a fruit cake cooked in pastry. Many on sale these days are decorated with sugar birds' eggs, flowers and leaves, and the words 'Mother' or 'Mothering Sunday' piped in icing. The edges of the cakes are often scalloped or twisted in an artistic way.

MOTHERING SUNDAY CUSTOMS

A *fig pie* is fairly easy to cook and would make a welcome change. Here is a recipe:

a pastry shell previously cooked
2 cups of cooked figs — these
   can be dried figs soaked in
   water overnight, and then
   cooked
¼ cup currants

¾ cup sugar
½ tsp mixed spice
1 tbsp orange rind
1 tbsp treacle or syrup
2 egg whites

Cut the figs into small pieces. Add currants, sugar, treacle, spices and rind. Separate egg whites from yolks and beat whites stiff. Fold these into the mixture and mix well.

Pour into baked pastry shell and bake in a medium oven 375°F or Regulo 5 for about 20 minutes or until golden brown.

Serve cold with whipped cream.
The making of *frumenty* is very simple.
Here is the recipe:

2 oz (50 g) clean wheat soaked in water overnight ½ pint (250 ml) milk	flavouring — spices, chocolate or raspberry or whatever you prefer 2 tsps sugar

Strain wheat grains from water and put into pan with the milk. Bring to boil and stir while simmering with wooden spoon, until milk has thickened. Then add the other ingredients and cook for another two minutes adding a little more milk if needed. Eat hot or cold. Another way to make frumenty years ago was to boil fat wheat grains in water until a jelly formed and then put the mixture into a large pot with milk, sugar, eggs and sultanas and lightly cook. The mixture was then poured into pie dishes and warmed in the oven to be served up on Mothering Sunday and throughout the ensuring week.

Gifts

Children might be encouraged to give a posy of wild flowers and grasses to their mothers on Mothering Sunday. All flowers, twigs and grasses can be treated to prolong their life as described in the section on May Day. To make an attractive posy dress it with foil wrapped around the stems and a coloured ribbon and paper doyley to complete the effect. Also of course young ones could be persuaded that their mothers ought to have special treatment — such as help with the chores and tea in bed, to make them feel 'Queen of the Day.'

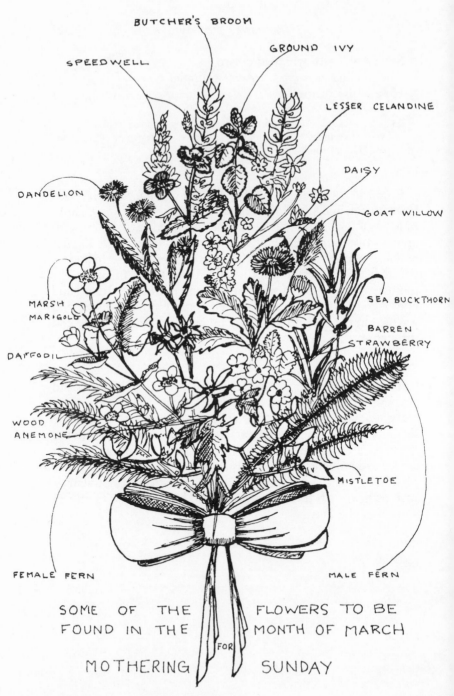

BUTCHER'S BROOM
GROUND IVY
SPEEDWELL
LESSER CELANDINE
DAISY
DANDELION
GOAT WILLOW
MARSH MARIGOLD
SEA BUCKTHORN
DAFFODIL
BARREN STRAWBERRY
WOOD ANEMONE
MISTLETOE
FEMALE FERN
MALE FERN

SOME OF THE FLOWERS TO BE FOUND IN THE MONTH OF MARCH
MOTHERING FOR SUNDAY

Mothering Sunday bouquet.

EASTER

Easter has been called 'The Queen of the Festivals' and in olden times people greeted one another on Easter Sunday with the words 'Christ has risen', and the answer came 'Christ is risen indeed'.

In the past the celebration of Christ's resurrection was regarded as the most important event in the Christian calendar — even more significant than Christmas.

The word 'Easter' is derived from the Anglo-Saxon word Eostre which was the name of a Saxon deity, and also Goddess of Dawn. The feast was held every year in the Spring — the same time as the Christian festival. So like most other ancient celebrations the two, pagan and Christian, were joined into one. The Saxon festival rejoiced in the rising and new growth of nature in Springtime after the death of Winter, and this corresponded suitably with the resurrection of Christ. Some people think that the name for the Christian festival was derived from the word 'oster' — which means 'to rise', and this also applies to the resurrection.

Eastertide is a movable festival and is not celebrated at the same time every year. People have often been puzzled as to how the date of Easter is determined in any one year. In an old prayer book the rule is given that Easter Day is always the First Sunday after the full moon which happens on or after 21 March. If the full moon falls on a Sunday, then Easter Day is fixed for the following Sunday.

The Jewish festival called the Paschal Feast was the Jewish passover kept on 14 April every year. Pasche eggs were well known in many parts of Britain over Eastertide and this is where the name springs from. Easter eggs and their story are dealt with later on.

Everyone knows, of course, the story of Easter, how Jesus Christ was deserted by his friends and crucified on Good Friday. And how he was lain in a tomb carved out of a rock and stone placed at the entrance to seal it off. In fact a guard was put at the tomb to see that no one stole the body. Early on Easter Day a small group of women went to the tomb to finish embalming the body, and found that the stone had been rolled away, and the body gone. Later, Mary Magdalene saw Jesus outside the tomb and mistook him at first for the gardener. The news spread rapidly that Jesus had risen from the dead, and people marvelled at this miracle. Jesus stayed with his friends another 40 days or so before ascending into Heaven. The resurrection of Christ forms the basic belief of Christianity — mainly that after death Christians being cleansed from their sins will rise again and ascend into Heaven, as Christ himself did.

Many of the Easter customs and celebrations have survived until the present day. Others, like so many associated with festivals have died out and are in danger of being forgotten forever. I have tried to include here some quaint traditions which are no longer practised, and I hope that you will be interested in them.

Holy week beginning with Palm Sunday precedes Easter Day. Apart from the obvious custom of gathering palms or other appropriate leaves and branches to remember the triumphal entry of Jesus into Jerusalem on that day, there were many other rituals. For instance, in Hereford pax buns and cider were distributed amongst the congregation in most churches after the morning service. The church wardens performed this act, and gave refreshment with the words — 'Peace and good neighbourhood'. Figs were popular on Palm Sunday and this needs no explanation. Fig pies and puddings were made and eaten, and a good quantity of dessert figs were also eaten. Fig fairs were held on the preceding day and large amounts of figs were displayed and bought. In fact, this day was often called Fig Sunday in many English counties.

In Shropshire on Palm Sunday many people ascended Pontesford Hill to look for the Golden Arrow. Mystery surrounds the origin of this custom, but it was believed that the Golden Arrow as well as being priceless, possessed magical properties, and the one who found it would become the owner of a powerful charm.

A wake, or large party was held on the brow of Pontesford Hill in days gone by and there was dancing and merrymaking, especially during the evening and no-one seemed to mind that the Golden Arrow had not been found after all!

The Wednesday in Holy week was often called Spy Wednesday in reference to the plot to betray Jesus. This day was also called Judas Wednesday and in some places Dark Wednesday.

Maundy Thursday

On Maundy Thursday the distribution of alms and washing of feet by the ruling monarch arose from Christ's act of humility when he washed the feet of his disciples. This custom was observed by many ruling Christians since that time but it was not connected with English royalty until Edward II washed the feet of 50 poor men on Maundy Thursday in 1326. Later, in 1361, Edward III gave 50 pairs of slippers to 50 poor men, and, as the age of the king was 50, this is where the custom of giving a number of gifts in accordance with the age of the monarch originates.

During Tudor times the Maundy custom was observed with much reverence and care. Elizabeth I washed the feet of the same number of poor women as she had years — (after they had been previously washed by a servant!) — and then distributed gifts of cloth, food including fish, and money during a religious service. Mary who preceded Elizabeth on the throne began the custom of giving her finest robe to the oldest women present. The religious Maundy service derives its name from the Latin word *mandatum* — meaning a commandment, and the opening words of the service have always been, 'A new commandment, give I unto you'. The Maundy Dish used in the ceremony bears the cipher of William and Mary, but does in fact date back to Charles II.

The washing of feet was discontinued around 1730 but the Lord High Almoner and his assistant are girded with linen towels in remembrance and carry the traditional nosegays of sweet herbs (thought to be effective in warding off disease in olden times). The pieces of linen used bear the date of 1883.

The Queen's Bodyguard, the Indoor Guard which forms part of the Yeoman of the Guard, is the oldest Royal Bodyguard and Military Corps in existence, having been created by Henry VII, in 1485. Preceding 1890 the Maundy service was held in the

Banqueting Hall in Whitehall, but after this date and up to 1952 the service was held in Westminster Abbey.

During the reign of the present monarch, however, the service has been held at Westminster Abbey on alternate years, and in the intervening years in such places as St Paul's Cathedral, St Alban's Cathedral, St George's Chapel Windsor, Rochester Cathedral and Durham Cathedral.

Some say that the word Maundy is derived from the maund or mand baskets used by the fisher-folk in Norfolk and Suffolk. Baskets like these were used for carrying gifts, and the monks used maund baskets to distribute gifts from early times on Maundy Thursday. Another explanation of the word comes from an old verb 'maunder' which means to wander or beg.

There was a famous fair held in Norwich centuries ago called Tombland Fair — on Maundy Thursday, horses, cattle and general merchandise were on sale. People including fisher-folk brought their maund baskets filled with items for sale — including the traditional fish. Many items of clothing were on sale including hats, in accordance with the tradition of wearing some new item of clothing on Easter Day. Many returned home with new hats — an industry introduced to Norwich during the Middle Ages. This may be where the Easter bonnet idea springs from.

Maundy Thursday was often called 'Holy Thursday' and in Staffordshire it was considered lucky to bring a piece of hawthorn into the house and keep it until Ascension Day. It was thought that such a deed would prevent the house from being struck by lightning. The old saying bears this out — 'Under a thorn, our Saviour was born'.

Good Friday

In contrast to all the other feast days of the year, Good Friday was a day of sadness and mourning. People were expected to attend church at least twice a day, and pass the rest of the day in solemnity and prayer. Shops, banks and law courts were closed, and this has been so to a certain extent up to the present day, although of course the habitual gloom of the day has more or less disappeared. The Anglo-Saxons called the three days before Easter Day, the Still Days, and they were so called because church bells were silent. The name Good Friday is probably derived from 'God's Day', but the Saxons and Danes called it Long Friday. Good Friday in Danish is *Langfreday*.

In modern times Good Friday is remembered primarily for the eating of hot cross buns. The custom goes back to pre-Christian times, when pagans offered their God, Zeus, a cake baked in the form of a bull, with a cross upon it to represent its horns. When the Romans settled down in Britain they also introduced the idea of making spiced buns marked with the sign of the cross. It is not known if hot cross buns were annually baked during Saxon times but it is recorded that a certain monk called Father Thomas Rocliff made some small spiced cakes to be distributed to the poor visiting the monastery at St Albans on Good Friday in 1361. The idea proved so popular that he performed this act every year, keeping his bun recipe a closely guarded secret. It is held that many tried to equal his success but no-one was successful. The recipe was recorded in Latin and the translation describes the buns as being small sweet cakes, stamped with the sign of the cross.

Throughout the centuries hot cross buns were made and eaten every Good Friday, and it was thought that the buns had miraculous curative powers. People hung buns from their kitchen ceilings to protect the household from evil for the year to come. Good Friday bread and buns were said never to go mouldy and this was probably because the buns were baked so hard that there was no moisture left in the mixture for the mould to live on. Hot cross buns and bread baked on Good Friday were used in powdered form to treat all sorts of illnesses.

A story from Warwickshire tells us that about two hundred years ago a small boy was suffering from diarrhoea on Good Friday. A neighbour prepared a medicinal mixture for the boy to swallow. This consisted of powdered Good Friday bread that was at least eight years old mixed with a little brandy. The mother was overjoyed when her son took the prescribed dose and became better in a matter of minutes.

Centuries ago many of the rich left their money or part of it to be distributed in some way annually after their death on Good Friday. Many unusual customs arose from this idea. For instance according to some legacies bread was baked and distributed to the poor of many parishes. In Lincolnshire in the parish church of Glentham there was a carved figure known as 'Molly Grime', and every Good Friday seven spinsters of the parish were ordered to wash the carved figure carrying water from a certain well two miles away. The terms in the will stated that after this had been done the spinsters would then be given one shilling each! This custom came to an end in 1832.

Years ago on Good Friday children in some parts of Liverpool would make and stuff a rag figure — something like Guy Fawkes, and visit houses early in the morning, waking up the occupants by knocking on the window with their dummy tied to a long pole. The figure was called Judas and the children would chant, 'Judas is a penny short of his breakfast'. This went on until 11 a.m. when the figure of Judas was burnt on a bonfire in the street causing much merriment, while the collectors enjoyed the sweets and apples bought with the money. Eventually because of the real danger of fire the police put a stop to this practice — much to the disappointment of the children in the area.

People were very superstitious on Good Friday, and it was considered next to Hallowe'en to be the most vulnerable day in the year, and the time when witches and evil spirits of all sorts did their worst. For protection many people cut branches of Rowan — the Mountain ash tree, and brought the twigs into their houses to guard against the powers of evil. It was believed generally that Good Friday was a special day for witches and that they would meet and exchange spells and secret rites, and plan evil. In 1633 a woman named Margaret Johnson was tried as a witch and confessed, or was tortured until she confessed, that Good Friday was indeed a day of peculiar importance for witches. This happened in Lancashire and it was reputed that the poor woman in question said that there had indeed been a meeting of witches at Pendle-water, before her trial.

Superstitions connected with the nails that pierced Christ's body on the Cross meant that blacksmiths refused to drive nails into horseshoes on this day, and lead miners would not work. Also, it was considered unlucky to stir or poke the fire with firetongs or metal pokers, and instead a piece of Rowan wood was used.

Cramp rings made out of metal from coffins or coins made the same way were worn on Good Friday many years ago as protection from cramp and fits. Henry VIII believed in this and carried out the custom, and even in this century it was reported that in Suffolk nine youths each gave a crooked sixpence to be melted down to be made into a cramp ring to be worn by a young woman liable to fits.

There were many other beliefs concerning this day. It was thought unlucky for fishermen to fish and for housewives to wash clothes. In the latter case it was believed that the clothes would be spotted with blood when they were hung on the line. In some places it was thought that the soap suds would turn to blood.

On the other hand it was considered lucky to plant potatoes, beans and peas on this day, and also lucky for children to be weaned. The breaking of pottery was regarded as a good omen as it symbolised the piercing of Judas' body with the sharp edges of the crocks.

As well as hot cross buns Good Friday was not complete without its boiled fish dinner. I well remember as a child having to eat this unpalatable meal.

In other parts of the country figs were eaten and at Brasenose College, Oxford, it was recorded in 1662 that the scholars ate large quantities of figs, almonds and raisins at supper time on Good Friday. In Cornwall saffron buns with clotted cream were consumed and in the North of England a herb pudding made chiefly from dock leaves and roots was eaten traditionally. The dock plant contains a large amount of tannin and was consumed as a protection against diseases, furthermore it is supposed to take on the shape of the cross when it reaches fruition stage.

Many churches erected the Easter sepulchre within their walls and arranged for the sacred place to be watched day and night from Good Friday until Easter Sunday. Candles were lit and were not allowed to go out until the ritual was over. In many homes too, fires were extinguished Easter Eve and then relit — the tapers being brought from the church candles. This custom was thought to protect the inmates from storm and disaster.

Games

Many games were played over Easter, and Good Friday was especially noted for traditional games such as marbles, skipping and tops.

We know that the game of marbles has been played since pre-

Christian times, although it was not called 'marbles' until the fourteenth century. Small stones, nuts or other round objects were used in the early days. The Roman Emperor Augustus (AD 63-14) used to play marbles with pebbles or nuts. Some people think that marbles are played on Good Friday because the game is linked with the dice throwing games played by the soldiers at the foot of the Cross. In the fourteenth century the game was played as a substitute for bowls and took its name from the material that bowls were first made of. Later offcuts and chips from marble were used to make the traditional 'marble'.

The game of marbles has been played on Good Friday at the Greyhound Inn, Tinsley Green, Sussex for centuries. There is a story that a local girl in Elizabethan times asked her various suitors to play a game of marbles for her hand on one Good Friday and this is where the tradition springs from. Sussex and other counties have a thriving marble league with teams with such entertaining names as Tinsley Green Tigers, Cherry Pickers, Bulldogs, Copthorn Spitfires and the Toucan Terribles. An annual marbles match is played at Tinsley Green on Good Friday, to establish the World Championship. In the yard of the Greyhound on a concrete sand covered circle six feet (two m) in diameter and standing two or three inches (six cms) off the ground, teams of six compete in this exciting event, 49 marbles are placed within the circle and the object of each competitor is to shoot his 'tolley' — a ¾ inch (two cms) marble and see how many of the other marbles he can knock from the circle while keeping his own within the ring. If he succeeds with his first shot, then he is allowed another turn. In this event the players must only grip their marbles between the forefinger and the thumb and shoot with only the thumb. If he moves any other part of his hand while shooting he is penalised for 'fudging'.

In 1976, after a run of 20 years as champions, the Toucan Terribles lost to a team of youngsters from Pittsburg called the Pernod Rams. The individual event to establish the supreme World Champion follows the team event. Len Smith of the Toucan Terribles has won this match 15 times but lost to his son, Alan in 1974. In fact Len Smith won the Championship 19 times in all. Since that time there have been a miscellany of winners.

Games of marbles include Alley, Bounce Eye, Dobblers, Five O's, Fortifications, Hundreds, Increase Pound, Knock Out and

Moshie. In the past home made marbles fashioned out of clay were used. These were called 'maradiddles' and a clay commoner was worth a one-er. 'Taws' and 'stoneys' made out of brown marble were three-ers. 'Alleys' made out of coloured glass so called because they were originally made out of alabaster, ranged from four-ers to six-ers. A 'blood alley' and an 'alley' streaked with red was worth anything from a twelve-er to a forty-eight-er. A marble made from agate was considered priceless! 'Maradiddles' have died out but new kinds are 'glasseys', stoppers from lemonade bottles, and 'steeleys', large steel ball bearings. One-ers, three-ers and so on depicted how many marbles had been knocked out of the ring, by the one tolley.

Marbles can be played indoors but it is really an outside game — the rough surfaces and weather conditions providing obstacles which add excitement and skill to the play. There seem to be two strains of thought as to how a marble should be played. The marble players at Tinsley Green flick the marble with the thumb, and this is called 'knuckling' or 'fulking'; in other parts of the country the correct way to play a marble seems to be to catch the tip of your right thumb with your middle finger, place a marble just above the first thumb joint, hold it into place with your forefinger, aim, and let fly.

While the men played marbles the women often took part in skipping on Good Friday. The activity can be traced back to early times, and probably the first ropes were tree creepers or hop vines. The game probably started as a simple contest — to see who could skip the longest without faltering — a pleasant way to learn to count in far off days.

Group skipping was popular over Easter and women used their clothes lines and skipped in the streets. The local monks often encouraged this form of recreation as not only was it good exercise but it kept people from indulging in more harmful pastimes!

Brighton was renowned for its skippers on Good Friday. The fisher-folk of the community especially delighted in this sport. They would bring their ropes from the boats and skips in the fish markets and streets of Brighton. If the weather was good there was even skipping on the beaches. The day was known as 'Long Rope Day', and it is believed that the custom sprang from the memory of the rope with which Judas hung himself. Group skipping at Brighton was continued until the second world war, when the closing of the beaches terminated the custom and it has never been revived. Also with the gradual increase in popularity of the motor car, street skipping was not encouraged.

Skipping is still used in football training and keep fit activities, but of course it is the girls mainly who have kept up the various games of skill and fortune which go with skipping. Rhymes and chants vary from place to place and include: Pepper, Salt, Mustard, Vinegar; Rock the Cradle; Chase the Fox; Visiting; Begging; Winding the Clock; Baking Bread; the Ladder — and so on. Winding the Clock means that the skipper turns round while skipping, Baking Bread means she picks up a stone, whilst up the Ladder means that the skipper turns round another skipper — and all in the long rope game.

Spinning tops were very popular on Good Friday, and have a long and interesting history. They were used by the ancient Romans and Greeks. Some people say that they were taken out on Shrove Tuesday and put away on Good Friday in any one year. Perhaps they were introduced during the solemn days of Lent to provide the children with a little light amusement. Children used to cry:

> *Tops are in, spin 'em agin;*
> *Tops are out, smuggin' about.*

'Smugging' is described as the legitimate stealing of tops if played with out of season. All toys which were made to spin on a point or peg were called tops, and in ancient times a dried eel skin was used as a whip or thong.

In the Middle Ages and perhaps before, each village or town had its own large top kept for the sole purpose of giving the peasants something to do to keep themselves warm on icy mornings, while waiting about for work. These tops became known as town tops, and were usually made from willow wood.

There are many kinds of tops — whipping, peg, humming (usually used for gambling), boxers (made out of box wood), mushrooms, racing, klondikes (big heavy tops), Japan tops which are very flat, French tops with a special fitting for string and many others. Some are beautifully decorated. You can buy clockwork tops which are wound up to make them spin or make a simple top using a cotton reel and skewer.

The whipping top is the most popular. The lash of the whip is wound tightly round the top and withdrawn with a smart pull. The top is kept spinning by whipping it at intervals. A well spun top hums and may even stay motionless as if it had gone to sleep — hence the expression — 'to sleep like a top'. It can be lifted on-to a spoon or even the hand with practice while it is still spin-ning. With a whip it can be made to do all sorts of tricks as racing over the ground or jumping into the air — racers, mushrooms and window-breakers are specially designed to do this.

Easter Sunday
Easter Saturday as well as being one of the Still Days symbolised the end of Lent and the fasting that accompanied it. Centuries ago this custom gave rise to much celebration, unfortunately almost forgotten now. In Dorset during the last century one of the remaining end of Lent customs was for a procession of boys to march around the villages carrying rough torches and a black flag and chanting - 'We fasted in the light, This is the night.'

Easter Sunday provided the climax to the Easter festival and joyful celebrations started early on this day, in fact with the rising of the sun. It was commonly believed that the sun danced for joy at Christ's resurrection at sunrise. To see this phenomenon people climbed great heights because they thought they could thus command a better view. The sun was reported to twirl round and round and occasionally jump up and down. People watched it through darkened glass — and were never disappointed, by all accounts!

On this day also children and some adults visited certain springs or wells and drank from them flavoured water. Cups were often half filled with water and then sugar added to make a sweetened drink. Sometimes bottles were filled with water into which had been placed pieces of sweetmeat or peppermint. The bottles were then shaken vigorously, and the water drunk with great pleasure. In some parts of the country this custom was called 'rinsing' and Easter Sunday was called 'Rinsing Day'.

It was always considered lucky to wear an item of new clothing on Easter Sunday. As I mentioned earlier, hats bought at Tombland Fair, Norwich on Maundy Thursday were worn for the first time on Easter Sunday. In other parts of the country new gloves were thought to be essential — or maybe just a new vest.

But, of course, the real tradition on Easter Sunday as far as children are concerned, is the giving of Easter eggs. This custom can be traced back far beyond the birth of Christ — as far back as 900 BC to ancient China where it is known that eggs were decorated and used in festivals celebrating the return of Spring and the continuance of life. To early man the egg represented the world itself. It held life within it, although a seemingly dead object, and was surrounded by mystery. The egg came to be regarded as a good luck token — bringing health and fortune to whoever possessed it. That is why from the beginning of time eggs have been given as presents in the Springtime.

With the advent of Christianity it was natural that the egg was then used to symbolise the Resurrection, and the custom of exchanging eggs at Easter was more firmly established than ever.

The art of dyeing and decorating eggs at Eastertide has been popular for many centuries throughout most countries of the world. Usually eggs were hard boiled being cooked in water into which various plant dyes had been added. The purple flowers of the anemone were used quite frequently and these stained the eggshells green. For this reason this flower is often called the Pasque Anemone or Easter flower. The blossoms of furze, broom, or whin produced a yellow dye, while cochineal resulted in a pink colour. Onion skins were often boiled with eggs to give colour to the shells.

In the North of England flower petals or leaves were wrapped tightly round the eggs before dyeing. The eggs were then tied firmly in a piece of cloth which was dyed with the egg. When the eggs were unwrapped the patterns of the leaves or flower petals could be seen, giving a delicate fossil like appearance.

Eggs were often drawn or written on after being hard boiled, and some were even painted with gold paint. When I was a child my father drew faces on breakfast eggs served up on Easter Sunday. He said that the hens laid face eggs on Easter Day, and it was many years before my brother and I tumbled to the trick.

Others drew patterns on eggs, before cooking, with candle grease. When the eggs had been boiled and coloured the pattern made by the grease showed white through the colour. Another way to decorate eggs was to scratch designs or pictures on them after dyeing, using a sharp knife, or metal skewer. Some European craftsmen became very skilled at this art and many wonderfully decorated eggs were produced.

The shape of the egg and its contents has been such a source of wonderment to man that it is not surprising that soon egg shapes were being made in many kinds of materials. Peasants made wooden eggs and carved and painted them with the utmost skill. Rulers, merchants and other rich men of long ago had eggs fashioned out of gold, agate, marble, glass and many other precious materials. Some were decorated with priceless jewels, others with delicately painted designs or pictures. Most eggs had a 'surprise' inside, and opened to show perhaps a scene carved out of ivory, or a painting, or just a precious jewel. Necklaces were sometimes made out of tiny egg shaped jewels, and egg shapes were used for scent sprays, liquor cases or needlework containers. These 'eggs' are now regarded as priceless possessions.

Of course some eggs were made to eat, and, before chocolate was invented, marzipan, fondant and sugar eggs were made with wonderfully intricate designs. The idea of making a drink from cocoa beans was brought back to Spain from Mexico during the sixteenth century. Later it became a popular drink in all European countries and was accepted as a social drink in the seventeenth century when chocolate houses sprung up in many towns in Britain. It was not until the nineteenth century that chocolate came to be made in solid form, so it is only in the last 150 years or so that Easter eggs have been chocolate eggs. Probably the first countries to do this were Italy, France, Holland and Switzerland where the making and decorating of edible sweet eggs has had a long history.

The first chocolate eggs were made by hand using tin plate moulds in separate halves. These chocolate eggs were huge glossy shells adorned with flowers of sugar icing and ribbons, and were very expensive. At the beginning of this century machinery began to replace handwork, and hundreds of eggs were produced in the time that it had taken to make one. Since then the popularity of chocolate eggs at Easter has grown enormously.

Some interesting customs using eggshells have grown over the years. For example shells thrown into wishing wells together with bent pins and pebbles on Easter Morning were supposed to make wishes come true. In northern Scotland boys made boats from eggshells and sailed them in the burns or ponds near their homes on this special day.

In Germany and later in the U.S.A. egg trees were made as a room decoration over Eastertide. These were rather like a spring version of the Christmas tree, except that the branches to be decorated were usually offcuts of trees still in bud — often birch. Eggs used in cooking were carefully blown or the shell broken into two. These were washed and dried and then carefully painted with all sorts of designs and pictures. The shells were then hung onto the tree to decorate their rooms over Easter. Another decoration using an egg shell was an Easter bird. A blown egg — usually a large duck egg or goose egg was used, and decorated with a feather design, this was then hung as a mobile.

Many games with eggs have been played at Eastertime throughout the centuries. Egg rolling is still popular in some parts of Britain, in Europe and the U.S.A. It is thought to commemorate the rolling away of the stone which closed Christ's tomb. From Sweden we have the story of the boy who in 1624 stole a coin from a Holy well to buy eggs for rolling. At once his hand became paralysed and his mother had to do penance in the same place before his hand was healed and he was able to play once more.

Coloured and patterned eggs prepared by children were rolled down hills or meadows, and it meant good luck if your eggs remained intact until the end of the course. Bad luck would follow if your egg broke on the way. In some parts of Europe the egg that rolled furthest was the winner over all. At the end of the game children sat down and ate their eggs.

In America egg rolling has been an annual event for 150 years on the lawns of the White House in Washington. On this day thousands of children are admitted to roll their coloured eggs against each other. No adult is admitted without a child. Another egg rolling contest is held in New York's Central Park. Children aged from five to twelve roll wooden eggs using wooden spoons across a certain piece of lawn, and the winners gain toys and cash prizes.

Other games included egg tapping. The egg was held in the

clenched fist and the end tapped against the egg of an opponent who held his egg in the same manner. If a child succeeded in breaking his opponent's egg then he claimed it as his own. This game may be the forerunner of the game of 'conkers' — as described in the Hallowe'en section.

In Germany an egg treasure hunt was very popular with children on Easter Day. Adults would hide many coloured eggs in a large garden or meadow, and the children hunted for them. After most had been found, the possessors of eggs of the same colour played a duel of egg tapping. The one who succeeded in breaking the other's egg took all the eggs, his own and his opponent's.

A curious bequest said to be very old was the distribution of 600 cakes with the impression of the figures of two women upon them every Easter Sunday to the parishioners who attended the parish church in Biddenden, Kent. Also 270 loaves and the equivalent of cheese was given. The legacy left to the parishioners of Biddenden included 20 acres of land — the rent from which paid for the food. The land became to be known as the Bread and Cheese Land. No one knows exactly who the benefactor was but an article published in the eighteenth century said that Siamese twins born in the area in 1100 were responsible for the legacy. The two women called Elizabeth and Mary Chulkhurst were born joined together at the shoulders and hips and must have been oddities until their death — no operation was possible in those days to separate them. Perhaps they gave the land in grateful thanks to the people of Biddenden for looking after them in their lifetime.

The Biddenden cakes stamped with two women motive are still distributed; they are rather hard, more like biscuits than cakes and are usually kept as souvenirs instead of being eaten.

Easter Monday
On Easter Monday and the following two days many games of sport were played. Football was popular but not played so much as on Shrove Tuesday. Bowls, like marbles, has always been considered one of the chief Easter games — but was often repressed to discourage excessive gambling. The game has been traced back to the thirteenth century and a manuscript of that

period in the Royal Library, Windsor, shows two players aiming at a small cone.

The custom of 'heaving' or 'lifting' on Easter Monday and Tuesday was observed for many centuries. The men lifted the women on one day, and the women the men on the other. The person to be lifted sat in a chair decorated with flowers and ribbons, while stalwarts of the opposite sex lifted the occupant high into the air. The chair was either turned round three times, or the operation was repeated three times. The rewards for the efforts of the lifters were kisses, hugs and gifts. The custom is supposed to symbolise the Resurrection in an odd sort of way, and it was supposed to bring luck to all people taking part. It has been said that in 1290 Edward I was lifted on Easter Monday by the ladies of the court, and that he paid them £14 for the deed.

One of the oldest Easter sports took place on the Thames and other rivers on Easter Monday. A pole was fixed into the bed of the river with a shield attached to it. Youths would then ride in boats without oars drifting with the current — until they reached the shield. The aim was to break their lance on the shield without falling. If they did fall there were many waiting to rescue them, as this activity was watched by hundreds of spectators. It was reported that in the twelfth century this sport was very popular and people crowded onto old London Bridge to watch it.

At Ashton-under-Lyne, Lancashire, the custom of Riding the Black Lad or Black Knight on Easter Monday is probably one of the oldest rituals ever remembered. On this day the villagers used to make up an effigy dressed in black, and seat it on a horse. The horse was then led around all the streets of the village followed by a large crowd. When the procession reached the old Cross in the Market Place the dummy was taken off the horse, and leant against the Cross. The crowd threw sticks and stones and lumps of clay at it until it disintegrated. The pieces were then burnt on a large bonfire amongst much merrymaking. Some people believed that the Black Lad represented a hated Lord of the Manor in years gone by, but in local records no such person fits the part. Now historians think that the destruction of the Black Lad is a replay of the ritual of destroying Winter — the season most hated by people of former times. It is reported that the dummy was often draped with holly, and this reminded me that one Shrove Tuesday the effigy called Holly Boy — a dummy decorated with holly was also burnt. Perhaps this custom too represented the death of Winter. The Riding of Black Lad was last performed in 1953, the coronation year, in pageant form.

Rabbits and hares have always been regarded as good luck symbols at Easter. The reason was that both species produced many litters in a year, and were therefore popular as fertility symbols. At Coleshill in Warwickshire it was said that if a young man could catch a hare and take it to the Parson before ten o'clock then he would receive a calf's head, 100 eggs and a groat of money.

At Hallaton in Leicester a traditional custom also concerning hares takes place every Easter Monday. This is the annual Hare Pie Scramble and Bottle Kicking. It seems that hundreds of years ago, a woman was saved from being gored to death by a bull on Easter Monday, by the running of a hare across the bull's path. She was so grateful that she bequeathed a piece of land just outside Hallaton to the rector on condition he had a hare pie made and distributed to the parishioners, and also a good quantity of ale. The rector carried out her wishes and he and his successors have held an annual Hare Pie Scramble and Bottle Kicking match at Hallaton on Easter Monday ever since. Before the freezing of meat became possible rabbit or beef was cooked in the pie as a substitute, as hares are out of season at Easter.

For many years Mrs Edith Payne made the hare pie and in present times Mrs Julie Allen has taken over the task. The ingredients include four lbs (two kg) flour, two lbs (one kg) lard, two hares, three lbs (one and a half kg) onions, seven lbs (three and a half kg) potatoes, and seasoning. (I have added metric equivalents). Mrs Payne knew just how to combine the ingredients to make a delicious pie. The tin in which the pie is cooked is 20 inches (51 cms) square and too big to go into the cook's oven. So after the final touches have been made the pie is taken to the Bewick Arms and cooked in the ovens there. At approximately 1.45 p.m. the pie, already cooked, is taken to the church gates in procession and accompanied by a brass band and a large crowd. The pie is then cut by the rector and distributed to the onlookers. Then at about two o'clock the Bottle Kicking match starts between Hallaton and the neighbouring village of Medbourne to determine which team is to win a barrel of ale.

There are three barrels in the contest — two full of ale and one empty. The barrels are in reality small iron bound casks and more suitable for kicking than bottles. One of the full barrels is placed on top of Hare Pie Bank where the match starts and the aim of both teams is to get the barrels over the respective touch lines. The Hallaton touch line is the brook to one side of the bank and the touch line for the Medbourne team is the hedge on the other side of the bank. It seems that any number of players can take part providing there is an equal number on both sides. The game is exhausting to say the least and often involves good natured fighting. The team to score the first touch with the first barrel gets the ale inside, and there is a welcome break. The empty barrel is then played for in the same way, and whichever team to kick or touch it over their own boundary first is the over-all winner and gains the third barrel which is still full of ale. The matches are often gruelling and may last for up to four hours. After the event the competitors and onlookers alike trudge back to Hallaton to recover and prepare for the annual celebration dance held every Easter Monday.

Some years ago certain people tried to put a stop to these rather robust events and suggested that the money spent could be put to better use and donated to a charitable cause. But the people of Hallaton would not hear of it, and as one joker said, 'No pie, no parson and job for the glazier'. The custom has been allowed to continue without argument ever since.

EASTER CUSTOMS
Recipes
Children might like to try this simple recipe for *Hot Cross Buns* from the *New World Radiation Cookery Book* although I can't guarantee that it is the same as Father Rocliff's.

Ingredients:

1 lb (500 g) flour	2 ozs (50 g) currants
½ teaspoonful salt	1 oz (25 g) fresh yeast or ½ oz
1 level teaspoonful of spice or	(12 g) dried
less	1½ ozs (40 g) sugar
2 oz (50 g) butter or margarine	½ pint (250 ml) milk
	1 beaten egg

Method: If using dried yeast mix with two tablespoonfuls of the warm milk, and a little sugar, ten minutes before starting.

Sift together flour, salt and spice. Rub in the butter and then add the currants. Warm the mixture.

Cream the yeast or yeast mixture together with the sugar, then add the egg and warm milk. Leave to sponge for about ten minutes. Mix the flour etc. with the milk and yeast to form a light dough. Beat well and leave in a warm place to rise until the dough has doubled its bulk. Turn onto a floured board, knead well and divide into 12 portions. Make up into rounds then flatten and taking a knife cut a deep cross into each one. Stand on a floured baking tray in a warm place for about 20 minutes. Brush tops over with a little egg or milk. Bake in the oven for about 20 minutes with regulo mark 6 or 400°F, until medium brown.

Chocolate Eggs — and Chocolate Egg-heads

Ingredients:
1 large egg
4 oz (100 g) bar of milk or plain
  chocolate
currants or nuts (optional)

Decoration:
paints, crayons, cotton wool
or paper for hair, egg cup,
or large sheet coloured tinfoil

As with all recipes it is advisable to try them out first, before letting children 'have a go.'

Method. Slice the top of the egg shell off the egg, making the hole as small as possible. Pour out the contents, and set aside for baking. Put egg shell into egg cup with hole uppermost.

Break up chocolate into small pieces and melt in an oven proof basin over a pan of boiling water. Children must be careful not to burn themselves. If you are making a chocolate egg to wrap in tinfoil then put a pinch of chopped nuts or currants into the empty egg shell.

Carefully, using either a very small funnel or a teaspoon pour the melted chocolate into the egg shell — as much as it will hold without spilling over the edge. Put egg into refrigerator or leave in a cold place to solidify the chocolate again.

If making a tinfoil wrapped egg, peel off egg shell when the chocolate has set, and wrap in coloured foil.

If an egg is being made leave the shell on the egg but turn the egg upside down in the egg cup so that the chocolate end does not show.

Decorate eggs by drawing faces, sticking on paper hair or cotton wool for moustaches or beards according to individual design. Children might even add paper ears, hats and collars — there is no end to the variety and fun to be had decorating one's own egghead.

As a present the egg cup must be part of the gift, as the egg head must have a stand.

Things For Children To Do
Dyed and decorated hard boiled eggs

Ingredients:	**Decoration:**
as many eggs as necessary	onion skins, flower petals,
1 pint (500 ml) water	cochineal or other colouring
2 teaspoonfuls salt	matter for dyeing, small
	leaves or flowers for patterns,
	pieces of clean white rag and
	string, paints and crayons,
	metal skewer

If the children do not wish to dye their eggs but just to decorate the natural coloured shell then the eggs may be placed in a small deep pan filled with salted water — the salt is to prevent them from cracking. Bring to the boil slowly and simmer for about 20 minutes. Take the eggs out of the water and when cold and dry begin to decorate. Dyeing eggs with flower petals or onion skins is a matter for trial and error. Years ago people used the brown outside skins of the onion, either in the boiling water or tied round the eggs to dye the eggs brown. Eggs can be dyed pink by adding a teaspoonful of cochineal to the water, and other colours can be used in the same way. Dyes from flower petals such as broom or anemones were common place and children could experiment with all sorts of flowers and leaves.

If a child wished to be more ambitious she could try patterning her eggs with a leaf and flower design. Some small interesting shaped leaves and petals are needed and a little flour paste. Arrange the leaves or petals around the hard boiled egg in a piece of clean rag and tie as tightly as possible with string without cracking the shell. Put into cold dyed water and boil for about half an hour. Leave in the water until cold and then unwrap the egg, cutting the string which will have become tighter. The egg should have leaf or petal patterns on it when the rag is removed, showing through the dye.

When children have successfully dyed their eggs then they can use paints and crayons to draw pictures or patterns on them. If they wish to scratch a design on them a metal skewer should be used but they must be careful not to press too hard or the shell will crack. The water dyes can be stored in jam jars with lids and used repeatedly.

An *Easter tree* would be very simple for children to make. All that is needed is a collection of washed egg shells of varying shapes and sizes. Some could be nearly whole from blown eggs,

Decorated Easter eggs.

and others can be saved from cooking or eating. The hard boiled ones would be the easiest to use because the shell would be more resilient. Egg shells may be dyed, colour washed or sprayed with gold or silver paint. Once the coloured base is dry then all sorts of pictures and designs can be drawn or painted a differing colour on the inside. Decorated shells can be hung with black cotton onto twigs, arranged in a heavy vase so that the whole arrangement does not over balance. The cotton can be looped onto the twigs and stuck with a dab of glue onto the egg shells.

Another idea is for children to make an *Easter bird*. A large blown egg shell is needed and if a goose or duck egg is not available than a large chicken's egg will do. Children will need to draw, colour and cut out on stiff paper a bird's head, wings and a tail — to the size that is appropriate for the egg shell. Before sticking them into position the egg shell should be painted carefully with a soft paint brush. If some small feathers are available they may be stuck onto the shell, and the paper shapes before fastening them into position on the shell. If all goes well a very presentable bird should emerge. Taking a long piece of black cotton loop it under the shell fixing it underneath with a dab of glue to ensure that the bird hangs straight. Tie the other ends of the cotton together and fix to the ceiling or a high object from which a mobile would look effective.

An ambitious idea would be to make a *surprise egg* like the skilled craftsmen did long ago. Some children might like to try this. You need an egg shell that has been broken into two fairly equal parts. When the shell has been washed and dried paint the insides with the same colour. When the paint has dried fit the two parts together and decorate the outerside of the shell as if it were whole. When dry, varnish over with a clear varnish to give a more permanent finish. Take off the top half and put a surprise gift in the bottom half wrapped in cotton wool. This could be anything small such as a chocolate or a ring or a chain necklace. A hinge might be made with some sticky tape, fixing the two parts together again at the back. An egg cup would have to be provided with this gift as the surprise egg must have a stand.

Children might like to make a simple *'rinsing' drink* of the kind I mentioned earlier. They need a bottle or jar with a screw top and a few boiled sweets or mints. All they have to do is to fill up the jar with sugared water and put the sweets in. Leave the

Easter bird.

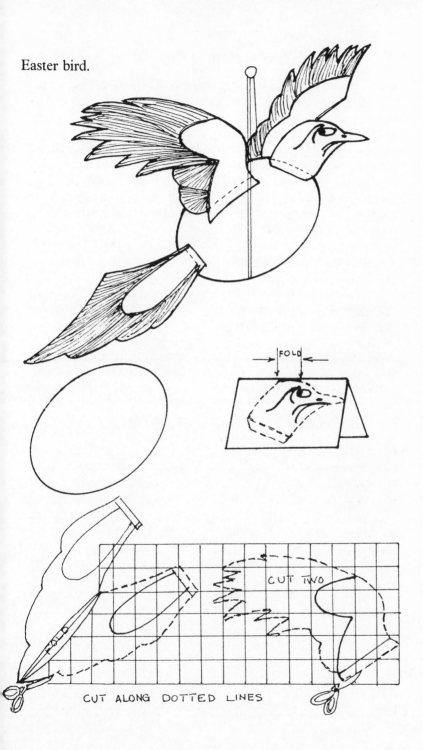

FOLD

CUT TWO

CUT ALONG DOTTED LINES

mixture for a day or so, shaking it vigorously three or four times, and after a while they have made quite a pleasant drink. The mixture was often coloured pink and always drunk on 'Rinsing Day' which is of course Easter Sunday.

When the children have boiled and decorated their eggs they may like to try out some of the egg games that were played years ago. Instead of playing 'conkers' with horsechestnuts children played *'Jauping Pasche-eggs'*. Two children have an egg in their hand which they protect as well as they can by curling their fingers round it. Each has a turn at aiming a blow at his opponent's egg with the hand that he holds his own egg in. If he succeeds in cracking the other's egg it becomes his property and vice-versa.

Egg races are fun and at a given signal children let their eggs roll down a certain slope and the one that crosses the finishing line first is the winner. The egg that rolls furthest also gains a prize.

A game mentioned earlier from Germany is for adults to hide eggs in the garden for the children to find. Once they have found them the pairs having the same coloured eggs play off for each other's eggs in a game of Jauping Pasche-eggs. A competition could be held to judge the best decorated egg.

Games

Children may like to revive some of the games that were played at Easter years ago. Skipping games and chants were popular and these are featured in A.B. Gomme's book *Traditional Games of England, Scotland and Ireland*. Spinning tops were in much demand and peg tops are easiest to handle. They are best spun by winding the cord of the whip two or three times around the peg before winding round the main body of the top. In the game Peg in the Ring tops are spun with a whip within a marked circle, and the aim of the game is to knock the other top out. A spinning top can split another top and if this happens the owner of the winning top can take the peg from the split top as a prize.

A game for two players is called Chip-stone. Two lines are drawn parallel to each other six feet (two m) apart. Each player places a stone on one line and aims to spin his top and chip the stone over the opponent's line. While the top is still spinning the player is allowed to lift his top in his hand and redirect it to the pebble. A good spin can result in three to four chips in one go.

The game of marbles is still universally popular. Children could play Knock-out or Boss-out. One player throws his marble as a marker and his opponent throws his to touch it or come within a hand's span of it. If he does this then he wins the marble. If he doesn't then his marble becomes the marker and so on.

Ring Taw is where each player puts a few marbles into a ring drawn on the ground. The players then take turns in shooting at marbles taking any which they knock out of the ring.

Bounce Eye or Bombers also features marbles being put into a ring. Each player stands over the area in turn with a marble held to his eye. He lets it drop onto the group of marbles and those he knocks out of the circle he keeps.

APRIL FOOLS' DAY — 1 APRIL

The first of April, some do say,
Is set apart for All Fool's Day,
But why people call it so,
Nor I nor they themselves do know.

This verse recorded in Poor Robin's Almanak in 1760 echoes the general feeling about April Fools' Day before and since. The origin of this 'fun day' when people are tricked by others or sent on foolish errands before noon and are consequently named April Fools, has puzzled historians from time immemorial. The first record we have regarding this custom was in 1698 when a note in Dawks' News-Letter for 2 April stated that 'yesterday being the 1 April, several persons were sent to the Tower Ditch to see the lions washed.' The Tower of London in the past housed a menagerie as well as prisoners of the realm. This seemed to be a well remembered hoax on this date as it was written in April 1860 in 'Notes and Queries' (11, 10, p.395), that several people bought cards at a penny each from a ballad shop in Seven Dials which they thought would admit them to the Tower to watch the annual ceremoney of washing the lions!

Other well known fools' errands years ago included sending an unsuspecting child to a shop for strap oil or a guttering peg or some elbow grease — all unknown articles. Also it seemed that pigeons' milk was in great demand at that time of year and children were often sent to farm houses to ask for this non-existent commodity. People were sometimes sent to a bookshop to ask for the 'Life of Eve's Mother' or the second edition of 'Cock Robin' or the 'Life of Adam's Grandfather.' Other victims were told to deliver a note to a certain person and when the recipient read the message which said — 'The first and second of Aprile, Hound the gowk (cuckoo) another mile,' the unfortunate messenger was then given the note back and told to deliver it to another perhaps living a mile away. It was probably some time

and many miles later before he realised that he was being made
an April Fool.

All Fools' Day as it was called years ago was, and still is,
observed in many countries in Europe and Asia. One theory as to
why it is so widespread is that 1 April marked the end of the
Spring Equinox, when fun festivals in many lands were held to
celebrate the period when the sun's rays fall vertically on the
equator and day and night are of equal length all over the
world.

A story which is said to originate from the second century
suggests that the annual custom of fooling people was practised
even at that early date. Apparently one, Byrrhaena, informed a
friend, Lucius, that on the next day the yearly custom of
entertaining Risus, the god of laughter would take place and the
god would be very pleased if he, Lucius, would attend and mirth
and happiness generally would increase. Thus Lucius duly
presented himself and was greeted with laughter and derision by
the other members of the party for falling for the trick.

In France an April Fool is called a fish — *poisson d'Avril* —and
it is the custom to send friends a dainty present made up in the
form of small fish. This takes the sting out of the April Fool
teasing.

British historians have put forward explanations as to why the
custom exists in this country. Some say it marks the end of the
New Year celebrations in the old calendar when New Year's Day
was 25 March. Others say that it is a remnant of an obscure
Celtic rite.

Local names for an April Fool can be found in different parts
of the country. In the Lake District he is an April noddy. In
Cornwall and the north it is guckaw or gowk — another word for
a cuckoo. In Cheshire it is April gawby or gobby or gob. If a child
in Cornwall succeeded in taking in another he used to shout after
him — 'Fool, fool,. the guckaw.' On the other hand if the person
resisted the trick he would say — 'The gowk and the titlene sit on
a tree, You're a gowk as week as me.' Titlene refers to a hedge
sparrow, a bird that has a similar life style to that of the
cuckoo.

Although the cuckoo was welcomed as a symbol of Spring by
our ancestors and the familiar 'cuckoo' call in April was a sign for
rejoicing the word 'cuckoo' came to mean foolish or insane in

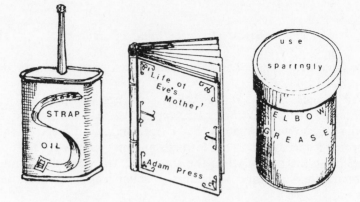

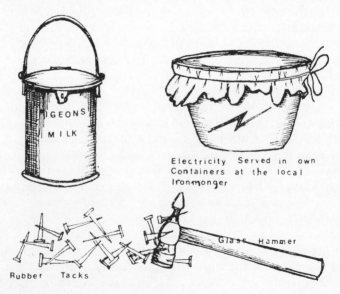

April Fool tricks.

many European countries. This may have been because of the bird's unusual nesting habits — namely it doesn't make a nest but lays one egg in another bird's nest, removing one of the eggs already there. The chick, on hatching, then proceeds to tip out the remaining resident eggs, so leaving the mother bird to bring up the 'cuckoo in the nest' as if it was her own. Perhaps this is one of the best tricks known in the world of nature. In fact the cuckoo is not necessarily the fool but rather the one who tricks others — depending on how you look at it.

As mentioned in my book *Origins of Rhymes, Songs ands Sayings* an old folk verse about the cuckoo goes like this:

> *In the month of Averil*
> *The gawk comes o'er the hill,*
> *In a shower of rain;*
> *And in the middle of June*
> *He turns his tune again.*

Also in the same book I tell of the 'village of fools' — the village of Gotham in Nottinghamshire, from whence stems the nonsense rhyme 'Three Wise Men of Gotham.' This village has many stories and legends attached to it which bear out this intriguing title. For instance it has been said that when King John was crossing to the west country with his private army he sent a messenger to Gotham to tell the inhabitants that he and his followers would be passing through their village. In those days it was the custom that every road the king trod would for ever more be regarded as a public highway. The people of Gotham did not want their privacy disturbed so sent a message to the king that they did not want him to pass through their village. This of course angered the monarch and he sent an advanced guard to investigate. The villagers fearing reprisals behaved like idiots and fools and their act so shocked the soldiers that they hastily turned back and reported to the king what they had seen. The village of Gotham was never troubled by royalty again. This story whether true or not must be one of the greatest tricks played on an English king but whether it took place on 1 April we shall never know. Another story about the 'village of fools' is that as the cuckoo was the symbol of Spring the inhabitants of Gotham grew a very high hedge around the parish boundary hoping to force the bird to stay and thus enjoy everlasting Spring. This, too, has links with April Fools' Day.

In modern times this 'fun day' is as popular as ever. For as well as the usual tricks played within the family or in the company of friends, radio disc jockeys have taken up the sport. For instance a year or two ago morning radio listeners were told in all seriousness that the day was something of a natural phenomenon and because of the unsual position of the earth in relation to the sun the powers of gravity were greatly reduced in some areas of the world. Patrick Moore, the well known astronomer gave a brief talk on this and said that as far as Britain was concerned the weakened gravity areas stretched in a band across the country. He asked listeners to try jumping up and down to find out if the forces of gravity had changed in their area. Then they were told to phone into the B.B.C. to report what they had experienced. Consequently hundreds of people from all over Britain spent the morning jumping up and down and then 'phoning results. Most said that they had been able to jump much higher than ever before and some said they had experienced a definite floating feeling. One man said that he was so buoyant that he floated up to the ceiling! Just before the show finished at noon the commentator thanked everybody for their co-operation and tremendous response in helping in scientific research. The signature tune of the programme played and then faded and someone said 'sotto voce' — 'April Fool.'

Another recent radio morning show at this time of the year was reported to be relayed — live — from an aeroplane. The small craft with appropriate background noises went through severe storms and every kind of weather hazard. In spite of the brave words exchanged between pilot and disc jockey that in any event the show must go on — radio contact was lost with the 'plane and apologies were made from the B.B.C. for the breakdown of the programme. Then the 'phone calls began to pour into Broadcasting House from worried listeners anxious to know the fate of the 'plane, passengers and crew. All turned out well and after a safe landing just before midday, the disc jockey, adhering to the tradition that he who plays jokes on April Fools' Day after 12 o'clock is himself a fool, announced with a chuckle that the whole operation had been a gigantic April Fool hoax.

As the old saying goes:

> *April noddy's past and gone,*
> *You're the fool an' I'm none.*

MAY DAY — 1 MAY

The May Day revels have existed from very early times and may be as old as the Harvest celebrations. They were indeed true pagan festivals that reflected the joy felt by the community as a whole that Winter had passed and Summer was officially welcomed at last. With the exception of Guy Fawkes Day, May Day tended to be the most boisterous of all the festivals. Youths and maidens went a-maying on May Day Eve into the woods and did not return until dawn on May Day carrying garlands of flowers, branches of hawthorn or blackthorn and usually a birch or pine trunk stripped of its branches — which was to become the village maypole. The cutting down and bringing in of the slim tree trunk to be erected and festooned as the centre piece for the May celebrations has strong connections with tree and nature worship. The myths and legends of pre-Christian Rome tell us that Kybele the goddess of flowers and fruitfulness had a lover named Attis, who by mischance was gored by a wild boar and bled to death under a pine tree. When Kybele heard this she was distraught but believed that the spirit of Attis had not died but had taken refuge in the pine tree. She therefore ordered the tree to be cut down and brought to Rome on waggons amid much mourning, exactly as if for a funeral march. She also ordered that the tree should be bound with linen and decorated with violets as they were Attis' favourite flowers. The tree was laid in a tomb and for many days there was much sorrow in the city of Rome — people worked themselves up into a frenzy of grief and cut themselves with knives — and this period was known as the blood days. Then on 22 March, the first day of the vernal equinox, Attis was resurrected and rose from out of the pine tree and was reunited with Kybele. Then of course came a time of great happiness and the garlanded tree was erected near the temple of Magna Mater on the Pantine. This festival was known as *Hilaria* and everyone rejoiced that Attis lived and so symbolised the rebirth of all living things in the Spring. The celebrations ended on 1 April and have strong links with April Fools' Day — and obviously everyone had a *hilarious* time. It is interesting to note that in the Lake District the practice of making people May geslings or goslings on 1 May is similar in practice to making an April Fool of someone.

The Spring festival became an annual event and soon every country in Europe and beyond was erecting maypoles in memory of Attis and Kybele and rejoicing in the rebirth of all living things. In northern Europe owing to the temperate climate and the calendar adjustment the Spring festival was held about a month later. Celebrations on 1 May continued thoughout the centuries and were enjoyed by all — from the ruling monarch down to the poorest labourer. It was reported that in 1511 and 1515 Henry VIII and Queen Catherine and the royal court went a-maying and the revels were most exciting!

When Oliver Cromwell seized power all festivities were forbidden and many old customs were forgotten, never to be revived. Nevertheless when Charles II — the merry monarch — came to the throne he was the first to encourage the restoration of all festivals.

The most famous maypole in England was erected in 1661 in the Strand and stood over 134 feet high and lasted for over 50 years. It was eventually felled and used by Sir Isaac Newton in 1717 for supporting Mr Huygen's reflecting telescope. Another maypole set up in Aldgate so overshadowed the south door of the adjoining church that it was renamed St Andrew Undershaft Church. Most of the village maypoles were taken down after the revelries and used as house beams or made into ladders. One of the oldest maypoles still in existence is at Hemsell in Lincolnshire where the ladder up to the belfry in Castle Bytham Church bears this message — 'This ware the May Poul, 1660.'

Although the maypole, often called the rod of peace, was extremely well decorated with painted spirals or horizontal rings and festooned with flowers and ribbons, it was not until late in the nineteenth century that the plaiting of the ribbons and the dances associated with it were introduced to this country. A school teacher from Whitelands College devised the ribbon plaiting dance that we know so well in modern times. Before this only ring dances such as Sellengers' Round were performed around the maypole.

One of the most important functions of May Day was the crowning of the May Queen and the May King or Green man —a relic of the Kybele and Attis myth. The ceremony which included a mock marriage symbolised the joining together of all living things and promoted fertility rites. Today it is only the May Queen that is crowned and she is chosen from the young girls in the community where she lives, for her beauty and personality. In many areas years ago, the May Queen's duties extended beyond May Day and she was responsible for attending events organised by young people throughout the Summer. Surely this tradition must have been the start of beauty contests as we know them today.

From first light on May Day the young people came into the villages and dressed doors and windows with garlands of flowers and may. Horns were blown echoing the pagan custom of welcoming in the Summer by the blowing of ancient Mayhorns at the time of Julius Caesar. More recently cow horns were used not only for blowing but for drinking out of too. Other musical instruments such as fiddles, drums and whistles were used to great effect in the May parades.

Children made May garlands out of hoops decorated with flowers, greenery and ribbons and hung a flower decorated doll from the central hoop — a small version of the May Queen. One type of May garland was in the form of a pyramid having three hoops attached to a pole, the smallest at the top — all expertly covered with flowers. Another which the boys usually made consisted of a miniature maypole — brightly painted and garlanded with flowers. Sometimes a doll dressed and arranged prettily in a box amid flowers would be carried round by the girls. People would then pay money to lift the napkin covering the doll and take a look — a custom which was supposed to bring luck.

Carols were very much in evidence on May Day and children went a-carolling around the houses singing special May songs and collecting money for their tea — usually held in the village school room.

Maidens prayed for a goodly fall of dew on May Day morning and all went into the fields and washed their faces in it. The dew was thought to contain healing properties as well as being a beauty cosmetic. May dew collected from grass, hawthorn and flowers early on May morning and rubbed into an infected part of the body was thought to effect a cure. In Launceston it was believed that a swelling on the neck would be cured if dew taken from the grass or flowers of the grave of the last person to be buried there was applied to the afflicted area. People suffering from consumption had their faces bathed in dew and all babies' foreheads were sprinkled with it to ensure health and good looks in future life.

In addition to the May King and Queen and the dancers around the maypole there was much more to be seen at May Day carnivals years ago. The Morris dancers, dressed in white suits and coloured sashes, straw hats, and festooned with ribbons and bells, carrying white handkerchiefs and the traditional sticks provided very good entertainment. Morris dancing has its roots in the mists of time and is thought to have started with the Sword dance — the oldest type of formation dancing known which went back to the tribal rhythmic movements interpreted as praying to the gods for rain or food. Although the Sword dance is now obsolete the Morris dance is still regarded as a popular event in modern times — due mainly to Cecil Sharp who at the beginning of the present century collected and recorded the tunes and dance movements of the Morris Men. The Morris dance may have been introduced to England from France or Spain, where country dances known as Moresco were performed, from the time of the twelfth century when the Moors were driven out of the Peninsula. The Morris Men use a variety of steps and dance patterns and flourish their handkerchiefs to great effect and click their sticks to keep a steady rhythm. Usually other characters accompany the Morris Men such as Robin Hood, Maid Marion (a youth in girl's clothing), Friar Tuck and Little John, the Fool carrying a bladder on the end of a stick, and sometimes a sword bearer carrying a flower decorated sword and a cake tin in which there are pieces of May cake. These are distributed on the tip of a sword to members of the audience, to bring luck. There is usually a fiddler playing the tune and the air most used is 'Green Garters'. Another theory is that the word Morris is derived from the French dance the Mauresque brought to England by soldiers who might have seen the dance during one of the early European wars. But most historians agree that the Moorish origin is the most probable as the dancers used to blacken their faces to imitate the Moors, and later disguised themselves as the tradition developed that Morris dancers should remain anonymous. Even today some dancers cover their faces with ribbons to conceal their identity. The most well known Morris dances are: Bean Setting, the Handkerchief Dance, Blue-eyed Stranger, Riggs o'Marlow and Trumbles.

Other pleasant customs practised by our ancestors on 1 May included the milkmaids' dance and the parade and dance of the chimney sweeps. The milkmaids decorated their buckets with flowers and adorned them with pieces of silver and plate lent to them by their customers. Then they put on their best dresses and 'kerchiefs' and with their buckets balanced on their heads did a charming dance outside each house where they delivered milk, and were given largesse or tips. The chimney sweeps with their blackened faces and costumes garlanded with flowers would dance through the streets banging fire shovels and brushes to attract attention. They were always accompanied by a man called Jack in the Bush who was covered in greenery from head to foot which some say represented the original maypole. Others in the party collected money for the sweeps.

In Cornwall May Day became to be known as Dippy Day as it was thought a crime if a sprig of hawthorn was not worn — and boys went around the towns throwing water over people who did not observe this custom.

The lighting of fires at this time of year originates from the Celtic custom, when the first fire festival of the year called Beltane was held. The purpose of the fires was to purify the earth and free growing crops from witches' spells. Bones were often burnt because the foul smell of the smoke was supposed to drive evil spirits away, and that is where the word bonfire comes from.

No May Day years ago would be complete without the parade of the Hobby Horse and his followers. A man dressed in a circular crinoline frame which covered most of his body and a horse-head mask together with his followers such as the Teazer, a Man dressed in a clown's costume and carrying a cardboard club, a man dressed in woman's clothing called 'All sorts', several sailors and the Fool of Whiffler with his bladder on a stick, would do a fantastic dance all round the village — the Whiffler clearing a path for them. The mini play and dance routine acted out by the Hobby Horse team has strong connections with early mummers' plays and may have its roots in animal worship. Padstow in Cornwall and Minehead in Somerset are two places where the Hobby Horse can still be seen.

The horse was certainly man's best friend, for not only did it pull heavy loads and plough fields but it also carried man from place to place at a goodly pace. May Day was known as Horse Ribbon Day in the northern counties because horses and carts were decorated with flowers and ribbons and joined the May Day parades.

Many games and sports were played after the May carnival. In some places the may garlands and decorated dolls were hung on a rope across the village street and children played ball over the rope. Other games suitable for children were blind man's buff, climbing the greased pole, conjuring and card tricks, all kinds of races, gymnastic displays, boxing and wrestling. Adults, too, joined in similar games such as bowls, 'escaping from the rope' tricks and archery.

These festivities developed into fairs and there were many held on May Day across the country. Mayfair in London takes its name from a fair held in that area over two hundred years ago.

Towards the end of the nineteenth century various Socialist and Communist parties in Europe gave the name Labour Day to 1 May and celebrated accordingly. Now in Britain, the first Monday in May is set aside for a Bank holiday.

MAY DAY CUSTOMS
Things For Children To Do
In addition to the crowning of the May Queen and the traditional ribbon plaiting maypole dance other activities which were commonplace years ago might be revived. Why not add to the May carnival by re-introducing the Hobby Horse, the Teazer, All Sorts and other characters as well as a team of country dancers? The Hobby Horse team is well described in Wright and Lones' book entitled *British Calendar Customs* and illustrations in the book are also helpful. It might be difficult to introduce Morris dancing to children and this depends very much on the teacher and the pupils.

On the other hand all could make *may garlands*. Three hoops graded in size attached to a central pole and small enough for a child to carry would make an attractive decoration. A fairly straight stick about two feet (60 cms) long would be needed by each child. Circles of wire, the smallest at the top and anchored to the stick by three nails could be fixed to make the pyramid and then bound with coloured paper or streamers. Floral arrangements and greenery if specially prepared would remain fresh on the pyramid all day, and could be fixed with cotton or sticky tape. All large leaves not bearing flowers such as laurels and ferns should be completely immersed in cold water for an hour or two before being used. Flowers with soft or woody stems such as buttercups, daisies, clover, may (hawthorn) lilac and marigolds and many others that can be spared should be picked early in the day and the ends of their stems crushed and then the tips plunged into boiling water for ten seconds. After this they may be put into vases of luke-warm water in the usual way for an hour or two before needed. Flowers with hollow stems should be plugged with a small strand of cotton wool. This treatment applies to daffodils, narcissus and similar flowers. Dandelions have an excess of sap and so the end of the stems have to be burnt before using — and poppies which may be used in harvest decorations should be dealt with in the same way.

Boys might enjoy making a miniature *maypole*, by painting a stick gay colours in a spiral design and attaching ribbons and flowers. The girls could add their favourite doll to the pyramid garland as a small version of the May Queen or perhaps dress it up with flowers and lay it on a floral decorated box as children did years ago. Competitions could be held for the best efforts.

There does not seem to have been many special foods eaten on May Day in former times, but I think a *Victoria sponge* with a maypole decoration on top would be appreciated. When the cake has been made and a filling used to sandwich the two halves together, cover the top with soft icing or butter icing coloured green (for grass) or whatever colour you prefer. A stick of seaside rock or twisted barley sugar pushed into the centre of the cake with strands of coloured coconut or liquorice attached to the top by icing would make an effective maypole. Eight jelly babies could be set at intervals on the perimeter of the cake with the other ends of the 'ribbons' fixed to them with icing to complete the scene. Ordinary narrow conventional coloured ribbons could be used, or wool if preferred.

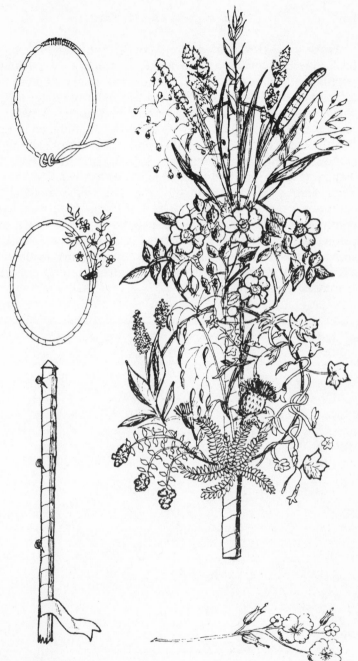

May garland.

Archery was participated in on May Day years ago. The sport has enjoyed a revival and to make an archery set might be popular with some children. To make a bow they would need to look for a 'bendy' stick, about two feet (60 cms) long, in the woods or by the river, a willow would be suitable. A piece of narrow elastic about 18 inches (45 cms) long should then be tied onto both ends of the curved stick and adjusted until the right amount of taughtness is reached. Any straight stick about 18 inches (45 cms) long and sharpened at one end would make an arrow and by trial and error the best materials for making an archery set would soon be found. Targets made of rounds of polystyrene approximately two feet (60 cms) in diameter and painted with appropriate rings and bullseyes would complete the scene. Outside archery competitions using home made sets would I am sure create excitement and interest among children of middle school age.

WHITSUNTIDE

Whitsuntide covers the period from Whit Sunday to the following Sunday which is Trinity Sunday. It is celebrated 50 days after Easter, and that means the beginning of Eastertide which is Palm Sunday. Better known is the fact that Whit Sunday is the sixth Sunday after Easter Day and also the immediate Sunday after Ascension day which is always on a Thursday. The festival of Whit Sunday commemorates the coming of the Holy Spirit to the Apostles which is described in the second chapter of the Acts of the Apostles in the New Testament. It also marks the official beginning of the Christian Church and Anno Domini (AD). Whit Sunday falls on the same day as the Jewish of Pentecost when Jews celebrate the giving of the Ten Commandments on Mount Sinai.

The term Whit Sunday is generally accepted to mean White Sunday, as centuries ago adults were baptized and confirmed at Easter and Whitsun — and they wore the traditional white robes. In Icelandic and Norwegian the literal translation of Whitsun is White Sunday and as these countries attained Christianity by way of Britain this seems a logical explanation.

Others say that the word 'white' remembers the tradition that on Whit Sunday the rich gave all their milk to the poor. Yet another interpretation is that as the old spelling of Whit was 'Hwit' or 'Wit' it referred to the giving of 'wit' to the Apostles on that day when they were granted the power to understand and speak several languages. A reference to 'hwitan sunnan deag' appears in the Anglo Saxon Chronicle dated 1067.

The churches were lavishly decorated with greenery years ago, just as they still are at Christmas in modern times. Historical records show that the secular celebrations at Whitsun were closely associated with the church. The wardens of most churches brewed ale at Easter and Whitsun in the church ale houses — for the enjoyment of the local community. They also provided food and after the strenuous activities and games played on this Bank holiday the parishioners would gather in the church hall and enjoy the feast. Special food was associated with this festival. For instance cheesecake and baked custard were eaten in many places and in Lancashire a kind of cake similar to a muffin was baked with a coating of white of egg and fine sugar on the top. These cakes were called Top Cakes. In Sussex the traditional dish was roast veal and gooseberry pudding and in Oxfordshire small Whit buns were made similar to the well known Banbury cakes.

People who could afford it paid for the food and the proceeds were usually spent on improving the social conditions in the parish. The poor did not pay rates so the Whitsun ale money took the place of this revenue. Also paid to the church at this time of year were the Whitsun farthings — sometimes called Pentecostelles, Smoke money or Smoke farthings. This was the rate residents had to pay if they lived in houses with one chimney or more. Competitive games such as wrestling, bagatelle and archery provided entertainment in which the parishioners took part and lotteries were held to swell the church coffers. Profesional entertainment such as the Morris dancers were paid for from the proceeds.

In Chester, Whitsuntide was a great event for the town as this was when the local guilds numbering about 25 in all each presented a play taken from the Bible and dramatised in a way that ordinary folk could understand — such as the story of Noah. These were the Mystery and Miracle Plays and lasted from about 1300 to 1600. The players were elevated so that they could be seen by a large audience and usually performed on a cart or waggon suitably decorated with ribbons and greenery. In 1906 the Chester council attempted to revive these ancient plays but after a reproduction of three the project was abandoned as being too costly.

Other attractions in Whit week were fairs, fêtes and pageants, horse parades and carnivals in which the guilds presented their floats. At Shepperton near Sunbury, Middlesex on Whit Monday an annual punting match was held and the winners received a guinea, half a guinea and a crown for coming first, second and third respectively. Other prizes were offered such as a pair of buckskin gloves to be wrestled for and for the girls a fine Holland smock to be run for — all with free entry. In Devon emblems were attached to buildings to signify certain activities. For example gaudily trimmed hats were hung up or worn in church and used to advertise the fact that wrestling would take place. Trees uprooted and placed next to thresholds of dwellings indicated that intoxicating liquour would be sold at those places without licence. Men climbed greased poles (often the maypole) to reach the prize at the top, or wrestled for silver spoons or hats while women ran for gowns or legs of mutton. It was the custom for young men to give their sweethearts fairings — consisting of packets of sugared almonds, spices or gingerbread-nuts.

In Cornwall similar games were played which lasted three days — and hats, money and gold lace were hoisted on poles and paraded round the towns as prizes for the games. On Whit Wednesday, the last of the festival days, a mock court was held and those who were found guilty of all sorts of fabricated crimes were sentenced to perform unpleasant tasks which produced much amusement amongst the onlookers.

In Gloucestershire cheese rolling games were held and cheeses were rolled down Cooper's Hill near Birdlip, the young men ran after them and those who managed to catch a cheese kept it as a prize.

In Whit week mainly on a Tuesday, club walks were organised and people set out to walk through the countryside dressed in their best clothes with coloured sashes and top hats and rosettes. They often carried banners or flags and usually walked to church in the same manner.

Every five years the scouring of the White Horse on White Horse Hill, Berkshire took place. During the last two centuries dozens of volunteers took part watched by thousands of spectators. The Cotswold games provide an interesting point. They were organised in the seventeenth century by one Robert Dover to be held on a wide expanse of ground near Chipping Campden. The sports' ground was called Dover's Hill and it attracted the attention of James I who allowed one of his courtiers to elevate the event and make it the best in the country. Endymion Porter, the king's man called the games the Olympics as they were played after the fashion of the ancient Greek contests on the plain of Olympia. The 'Olympic games' were held every Whitsun until they were disbanded during the reign of George III.

At Lichfield, Staffordshire a Green Bower Feast was held every Whitsuntide, commemorating the granting of a charter to that city in 1549. Members of the council took garlands of flowers up to a hill outside the city where a large green bower had been erected. There everyone had a good feast provided by traders who sold all kinds of food including gingerbread and fruit. Later this was developed into Lichfield fair with all the normal attractions of stalls, swings and roundabouts.

A curious custom relating to the boys of Eton school at this time of year was the Montem. A procession of sixth form boys smartly dressed and accompanied by younger boys as their servants went to Salt Hill to collect 'salt' money which was then presented to the head boy — Captain of the Montem. The money was to buy salt for the school meals. Later the boys wore fancy dress and one was the Ensign and carried the flag. They collected money over a wide area but not over the boundary, and sometimes the collection amounted to over £1000. This custom is said to have connections with the Boy Bishop ritual which I mention in the section dealing with Christmas. The Montem was abandoned during the last century.

On the whole games and revelries held at Whitsun were much better organised than on other festival days. Nowadays of course the church observes Whit Sunday as always but Whit Monday has been replaced by a Spring Bank holiday not necessarily on the same day. Perhaps some of the customs practised at Whitsun could be transferred to the new Spring holiday.

WHITSUNTIDE CUSTOMS
Things For Children To Do
With the co-operation of the local vicars it would perhaps be a good idea to re-introduce the idea of garnishing the churches with greenery at Whitsuntide. Children would, I am sure, be very willing to help with this. Also village halls or classrooms, where Whit festivities were to be held, would look attractive decorated in the same manner.

An open air *play* staged by the children and performed on a decorated farm waggon would create much interest — as did the mummers' plays of years ago. I am sure a float left over from a carnival would be lent gladly by a local firm if no waggon was available.

Many communities already have fêtes and sports organised for most Bank holidays and a revival of some of the older customs might be popular. Why not call them the 'local Olympics'? For instance *walks* could be arranged especially for the children and they could dress up and wear hats and carry flags. Perhaps a charity collection could be organised and maybe the 'Hat Walk' would become an annual event once more.

Competitions including the making of *hats* would provide amusement. The children entering to be given identical materials and set time to make their creations. They might enter the contest in pairs — one to make the hat and one to wear it. The idea of wearing new hats at Whitsun may be connected with the Easter bonnet custom as the two festivals were closely linked.

Regarding the special holiday tea it would be of interest to all if some of the recipes used years ago were revived. *Banbury cakes* from Oxfordshire would make a welcome change and if cooking facilities were available perhaps children could make the cakes themselves.

Here is the recipe for Banbury cakes.

Ingredients:

½ lb (220 g) frozen puff pastry
1 oz (25 g) butter or margarine
2 ozs (50 g) sugar
½ an egg

1 oz (25 g) cake crumbs
2 ozs (50 g) mixed peel
4 ozs (100 g) currants
a little spice

Method. When the pastry has thawed completely roll out to one-eighth of an inch (three mm) thick. Cut into rounds of six inches (15 cms) in diameter. Beat up the egg. Beat the butter and sugar to a cream, add half the beaten egg, crumbs, chopped peel, currants and spice. Put a little on each round of pastry and add to the rounds until all the mixture is used. Wet the edges of the pastry and gather together at the top and seal carefully making sure all the mixture is enclosed. Turn the cakes over so as the smooth side is upwards and press out a little. Brush over with water and sprinkle with sugar and bake for 20 minutes or until golden brown at Regulo mark 6 (gas) or 400°F (electric).

HARVEST

Many centuries separate the early gatherers of wild wheat from the modern farmers with their combine harvesters. Wheat has been cultivated for thousands of years, and indeed some wheat grains found in a jar in an Egyptian tomb have been dated as early as 6000 BC. From the beginning of time man has needed security, particularly as the fight for survival was long and hard through many centuries. The pagan customs and rituals practised in conjunction with the seasons gave men the feeling of continuity and comfort that they so badly needed. They were a kind of insurance against the perils of an untamed world.

Of all the seasonal festivals Harvest was undoubtedly the most important. It was thought that the corn mother or earth goddess controlled the seasons, all forms of nature and symbolised the continuance of life itself. If the harvest was good it meant that the corn mother was pleased and there would be food to last the Winter. If the harvest was scanty the corn mother had been vexed, and famine and death would follow. In various parts of the world the corn mother had different names. In Greece she was known as Demeter, and pigs were sacrificed on her behalf. The Romans called her Ceres, and grain crops have been called cereals ever since. In Britain she was known as the 'White Lady of Death' or 'Life' or 'Inspiration'.

When the grain was ripe it was essential to gather it in as soon as possible while the weather was favourable, and so everyone who was able helped in the fields. One man was appointed Lord of the Harvest and he led the line of men cutting an armful of corn with a sickle as they moved up the field. Behind them men and women gathered up the cut corn and bound it into sheaves. Then other women and the children set the sheaves up on end and leant six or so together to make a stook so the wind could dry the grain.

When the corn was dry it was loaded onto waggons and stored in barns, the threshing not being carried out until the Winter.

When the last sheaf had been gathered the poor people of the community were allowed into the field to glean, and all grain they found, they were allowed to keep.

The last waggon load of grain brought in was held to be particularly important and was often called the Horkey or Hock cart. The waggon was decorated with flowers and ribbons and the horses also. The top sheaf — the last to be gathered — was arranged to look like a woman, probably the corn mother. Labourers walked beside the cart cheering and the whole ceremony was carried out with the utmost enjoyment. From the sheaf on top of the load, corn dollies were made, and this tradition can be traced back to very early times. They were made to represent the corn mother — although not very often as a 'dolly'. Different localities developed different symbols: Devonshire developed the Harvest Cross, Cambridgeshire the Bell, the Welsh borders the Fan, Hereford and Norfolk the Lantern and Suffolk the Horseshoe. People thought that the corn spirit lived in the last sheaf and so to preserve it and allow it to be reborn the next Spring they made idols out of the corn and brought them into the home. Here they were hung up in the kitchen where they served to protect the household throughout the Winter months from evil spirits and pestilence. The simple derivation of corn dolly is 'Idol of Corn'.

It is well known that the life of the farm labourer and his family was very hard and conditions did not alter for centuries. The work was extremely arduous and only 'starvation' wages were paid. After the wearisome toil of the year Harvest time was a time of merry-making and relaxation. The farmer gave a fine Harvest supper to his workers and their families and food and beer were in plentiful supply. Indeed the farm labourer probably only tasted meat twice a year — at Christmas and Harvest time.

Many customs were linked with Harvest home suppers, and they differed in different parts of the country. In Sussex harvesters used to put a lighted candle in a glass of beer and drink while holding the candle in position with the nose. The audience sang, 'Your nose is alight, your hair's alight. Afire.' Often the candle slipped from an over-heated nose and singed the drinkers' eyebrows. Another trick involved a man drinking a glass of ale, placed on the crown of a top hat, without spilling a drop. When he had finished he had to toss the glass in the air and catch it in the hat as it fell. In Norfolk there was a special brew called Horkey beer and this was drunk freely and with relish — to 'chase the old fox' (the tongue), 'down the red lane' (the throat). Here, too, was the tradition of a person trying to drink beer while his neighbour joggled his arm and did his best to make him spill it. He would sing, 'So lift up your elbow and hold up your chin and let your neighbour joggle it in'. Part of the entertainment was when one of the reapers chosen as Lord of the Harvest terminated his office by retiring from the room and returning dressed in a kind of mummer's robe. He would then call for largesse and the money collected was divided amongst the workers to help see them through the Winter.

After the Harvest ceremonies the time for wages to be paid came at last. The workers dressed in their second best would gather in the barn, and the farmer in a benevolent mood would tick off their names in his large accounting book and give out the money. A labourer might earn as much as £4 or £5 at Harvest time which was often paid out in gold sovereigns called Hossmen as they showed a picture of St George riding on a horse, and the dragon.

Much of the money earned at Harvest time and meant to be used sparingly throughout the Winter to support families when there was little or no work to be had, was spent, regrettably, in the ale-houses — resulting in much hardship. It was not until the middle of the last century that enterprising vicars began to encourage people to come to church, bringing Harvest produce to be blessed in a Harvest Thanksgiving Service. This custom proved very popular and was soon accepted as part of the Christian calendar. Not only did it prevent wages being wasted but it brought a religious element to Harvest customs which had hitherto been lacking. The Harvest Home suppers are no more but the splendid Harvest Festivals held in churches all over the country are still very well attended. Even the fishermen have their own special thanksgiving 'Harvest of the Sea' services held in churches akin to fishing ports. In addition to the fruits of the land the churches in these areas are decorated with fishermen's nets, lobster pots and ships' lanterns.

In modern times in addition to the Thanksgiving services held in churches, many schools hold their own Harvest Festivals —

and following the old tradition the produce is distributed afterwards to hospitals or families in need.

HARVEST CUSTOMS
Things For Children To Do
Simple *murals* or *collages* representing Harvest time would be greatly appreciated by pensioners or hospital patients and would of course look attractive as wall designs in or out of school. Straw has many uses and is easy to handle. If you do not live in a rural community where a supply is easily obtainable then most craft shops sell it. Apart from using the actual seed heads and stalks arranged in an attractive posy design and stuck onto a backcloth of coloured paper, there are other ways in which straw can be used. Effective 'match stick' people, houses with 'thatched' roofs, swings, see-saws, slides can all be glued onto a backing paper to make unusual collages — in fact there is an enormous range of pictures that could be produced, giving all children a chance to experiment and try out new ideas of their own. The old harvest scene using some straw with the seed heads still attached to represent the uncut wheat, short stalks for the stubble, and match stick straw reapers would look especially good against a background coloured yellow for the field, and blue for the sky above. For a more professional effect different shades of straw might be purchased and these arranged so as to give depth to the picture.

To remind people of the often forgotten Harvest of the Sea a communal collage using straw, milk bottle tops and pieces of small mesh nylon fruit netting, might be attempted. With a group of children each could take on a different task. First on a large piece of white paper draw, in the middle of the paper, the outline of the side of a rowing boat and leave white. Then paint a background of blue sea with white crested waves and a paler blue sky. Then when dry the boat may be filled in with glued lengths of straw lying horizontally to represent the timbers and the shape of the craft also outlined in straw. The top halves of one or two fishermen complete with sou'westers could be drawn, coloured, and cut out on separate pieces of paper and then stuck onto the picture so they appear to be leaning from the boat with hands outstretched. Milk bottle tops (washed and flattened) could be shaped in the form of fishes and put in a piece of net which should be stuck onto the side of the boat in such a way that the bottom is still in the water. Now we have a picture showing the fishermen leaning forward and drawing in their nets laden with fish. A title such as 'Harvest of the Sea' could be fashioned in straw and stuck to the top of the collage.

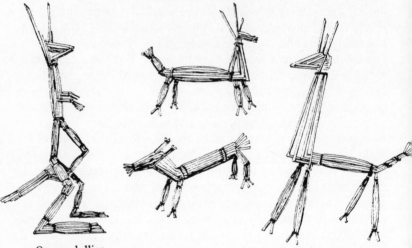

Straw dollies.

Another way to use straw and seed heads is for children to make simple *corn dollies*. Not the traditional designs using the complicated plaiting routine which was used in the ancient craft but rather figures and animals made out of strands of straw and grain and tied together with raffia. Before beginning, all straw should be soaked in water to make it more pliable. Several long stalks of equal length should be bound at each end, with the grain heads left on, to make effective heads, trunks and limbs. When these little figures are dressed in simple shifts and a paper face drawn, cut out and stuck onto the head they make attractive corn dollies in their own right.

Figures from straw can also be made by selecting about 20 lengths 10 inches (25 cms) long and binding these with raffia about an inch and a half (four cms) from the bottom. Then holding the binding pull the rest of the straw over the knot and then bind again to form the head. Push straw up and bind for waist. Take about six straws six inches (15 cms) from the end to

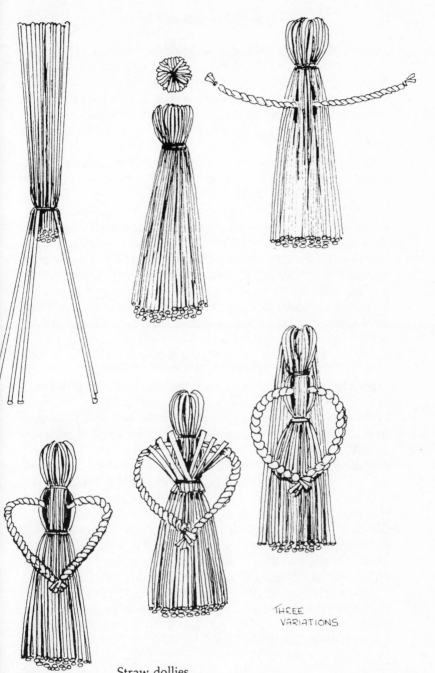

THREE
VARIATIONS

Straw dollies.

form hands. Attach with raffia to the neck and pull out the rest of the straw to form a skirt. A face can be drawn and stuck on the head, and the body can be dressed. Animals can be made in a similar manner with perhaps an ear of corn for a tail and ears of corn for realistic ears or horns. Afterwards the children might like to hang up their corn creations in the kitchen in the traditional way.

Adults who would prefer to make the *true corn dollies* need not despair. In recent years this ancient craft has been revived and is now taught in craft centres and evening classes. And every library has at least one book explaining the intricacies of the art. To make a corn dolly long pieces of straw are essential and the straw must be hollow and pliable. The use of artificial fertilisers tends to make the modern product too brittle for this craft and therefore special straw has to be obtained. A long stalked variety of wheat called Triticium is specially cultivated for corn dolly making and can be bought in most craft shops. On the other hand if you live near a field of wheat you may be lucky and be able to cut suitable straw.

In America dolls are made out of the sheaths of maize or corn cobs, and this art is called corn shuckery. The shuck being the American name for a sheath. The leaves of the sheath are peeled from the cob and dried until straw coloured. Using this material as the main component, Americans make not only dolls and animals, but models of covered wagons and whole families of settlers.

Apart from the usual fruit and vegetable gathering at Harvest time children could be encouraged to pick blackberries and make *bramble jelly*. To a pound (500 g) of blackberries put about a third of a cupful of water and let the fruit stew for about twenty minutes. Then add a pound (500 g) of sugar and bring to the boil and simmer for about another ten minutes or until the jam has jelled. Then pour into a small mesh sieve and, over a basin, rub the jam with a wooden spoon until all that is left are the pips. Pour the jelly into small jars and seal in the usual way. These pots of bramble jelly would make a welcome contribution to the Harvest Festival or could be given away by the children as gifts to relatives at Christmas time.

HALLOWE'EN — 31 OCTOBER

Of all the days in the year Hallowe'en — 31 October is perhaps the most exciting — our ancestors thought so, anyway. This was the night of the supernatural — the last fling of those who possessed magical powers before the Holy or All Hallows Day, which was to follow on 1 November, now called All Saints Day.

Not only was it thought that witches abounded, casting their evil spells on everyone in their path, but it was believed also that humans themselves could perform magic, see into the future and summon ghosts and other spirits to appear at will. Nowadays fewer people believe in witches and other magical beings but all the same many follow the tradition of telling ghost stories on this special night.

Hallowe'en was originally the second of the two Celtic festivals. Beltane was held in the Spring and celebrated the renewal of growth, and the continuance of life, while Hallowe'en or Samhuinn, which is the Celtic name and means 'Summer's end', celebrated the gathering in of crops and expressed to the pagan gods the thanks of the people for a good harvest to see them through the Winter. Samhuinn was in fact the eve of the Celtic New Year, and was celebrated in the same way as we celebrate New Year's Eve, or Hogmanay as it is called in Scotland.

The Celts also thought that Hallowe'en symbolised the Festival of the Dead. November was associated with death and decaying vegetation and the approaching long dark nights of Winter, and as the rituals of the Druids, the Celtic priests, were based to some extent on the pattern of Nature, the human life span was also associated with this. As natural life returned to the world in the Spring, so the Celts believed that the human dead rose again, and were resurrected in the same way. Therefore the festival of Hallowe'en was not entirely one of sorrow but only part of the cycle of life. The Druids performed sacrifices and offerings to the gods on Samhuinn as thanksgiving ceremonies.

In the off shore islands of Scotland and England such as the Isle of Man, the Romans and Saxons did not trouble to invade and so the Celtic way of life and beliefs were allowed to carry on undisturbed. In fact up until the beginning of the eighteenth century children dressed as mummers in the Isle of Man, and went from house to house giving entertainment on Hallowe'en celebrating 'New Year's Eve'.

In ancient times all over Europe people believed that the souls of the dead revisited their relatives on Hallowe'en. Perhaps this belief sprang from the fact that people thought that ghosts, fearful of the rigours of Winter, came to see their families to warm themselves by the fire and partake of some refreshment to help them face the cold and loneliness of the next few months. Many people in Britain left the table laid with food upon it, and the door unlocked before retiring to bed so that the departed could come in and take what they wanted during the night of 31 October.

An interesting story comes from the island of Barra about an incident that happened a few years ago. Apparently a visitor was staying on the island over Hallowe'en when some fishermen approached him saying, 'We have no false faces (masks) this year and there are none in the shops'. The visitor who was a writer collecting material for his book, made masks out of material and painted faces on them. They were truly grotesque and the fishermen put them on and danced with glee. They insisted that the visitor wore one too, and then presented themselves at a number of houses, at each one the inmate screamed with fright until the masks were pulled off, to be followed by screams of laughter. After a while it was decided that the maskers should visit a man who lived on his own in a 'black house' on the other side of the island. He was great in stature and a loner, and was held in awe by the local people. The group approached the house and the visitor knocked at the door, not realising that all the others had run away. He stood there wearing his mask, and when the owner opened the door, he showed no surprise but took the hand of the stranger and led him to sit by the fireplace. The householder brought food and drink to the visitor and behaved in a very hospitable way without saying a word. The stranger began to feel uneasy, and after a while took off his mask — making his host start back, his face going ghastly white.

'Did you not know me?' asked the stranger. 'No', said his host slowly, 'I thought you were ——— a ——— dead ——— man'.

The custom of entertaining the dead explains why ghost stories are so popular and later, when witches and warlocks entered popular mythology they too were associated with this 'magical' night.

When the Romans invaded England, the surviving Celts retired to the hills and swamps where the invaders did not dare set foot. The Celts became known as the 'little people' — certainly they were small in stature. They possessed a wide knowledge of herbs and poisons which were unknown to the Romans. The Celts used poisoned arrows, while out hunting, and these small flint arrow heads can be seen in museums today and are called fairy arrows. Stories grew up amongst the more civilised communities that the 'little people' possessed magical powers. Also they knew every inch of the hills and woods and could vanish without trace when pursued. This added to the growing feeling that they were truly supernatural, and this is where the image of the goblin, fairy, elf, kelpie and all the other magical beings had its roots. The Saxons, too, left the 'little people' alone.

Although not all spirits were thought to be evil by the superstitious communities of long ago, they were all held in dread and the thought of going out after dark alone on Hallowe'en was unthinkable in those days. In Scotland there was a belief that those who had been snatched to fairyland could be brought back to earth on Hallowe'en by the recitation of a spell in a certain 'fairy place'. Sir Walter Scott tells a story of a wife who was 'taken' by the fairies and who reappeared to her farmer husband in a dream, telling him to recite a certain spell at Hallowe'en, and she would be returned to him. He duly went to the spot after dark on the night and sure enough heard the passing of the fairies and the tinkling of their bells, but was so confused and frightened by it all that he did not recite the spell in time and so his wife was lost to him for ever. Another belief from Scotland was that between sunset and cockcrow on Hallowe'en it was possible to gain an entrance to a fairyhill by going round it nine times and then a door would open and admit the visitor to the fairy world.

The number nine seems to figure importantly at this time of the year. From Sir Walter Scott's *Waverley* we have this couplet:

For on Hallowmas Eve the Nighthag shall ride,
And all her nine-fold sweeping on by her side.

As previously mentioned the popular image of the witch took hold during the Middle Ages. With her black cloak, tall black hat and hideous face, not to mention her broomstick, black cat and dreaded spells she soon became the principal supernatural character on Hallowe'en. It was sincerely believed by people of former centuries, that witches and warlocks roamed the country freely after dark on their broomsticks, egg shells or sieves, or galloped along roads mounted on tabby cats transformed for the night into coal black steeds. Their favourite meeting places we are told were on lonely sea shores, moors, Druids' rings or churchyards. Robert Burns in his famous poem 'Tam O' Shanter' describes vividly the feelings and imagination of the peasants and what they thought happened when witches occupied churchyards on Hallowe'en.

In Lancashire it was generally believed by local people that witches met at every Hallowe'en at a place called Malkin Tower which was a ruined farmhouse in the forest of Pendle. The local performed a ceremony called 'Leeting the witches', and it was believed that if a lighted candle was carried about the fells near Malkin Tower between 11 o'clock and midnight and the flame burnt steadily, then the witches would lose their power and vanish. If the candle flame went out, however, then the carrier could expect ill fortune, as it was thought that the witches did their best to extinguish the candle flames during that time. Only the most stalwart of the locals would venture out to test this ritual. Others felt more secure by taking a fiery brand and waving it vigorously about, believing that this was a more positive way to scare witches away for at least another year.

In Britain, rowan, the wood from the mountain ash tree was thought to give protection against witches. A legend about a plough boy and a witch states that: a good and trustworthy plough boy was given a whip with a handle made out of rowan wood by his master. The farmer said that it was to give him and the horses protection against evil spirits, and was not to be used on the horses. The boy therefore carried the whip with him as a kind of lucky mascot. One evening on the 31 October, the boy was doing some winter ploughing on the field furthest from the farm house. It was dusk and he and the horses were tired, but there was only one more furrow to finish, and the boy encouraged the horses to make one last effort. The job was almost completed when suddenly from out of the hedge appeared a witch. She was dressed in black, crouching with her ugly face turned upwards towards the boy. She pointed a crooked finger and called, 'I've got you my pretty— now for my Hallowe'en curse.' But before she could utter another word the boy took hold of his whip stock and shook it at her and touched the horses for luck and protection. The magic of the rowan was so great that the witch cowered and stepped back, throwing her arms up to protect her face crying:

'Damn the lad with the rowan tree gad'. (handle). The witch vanished and the plough boy returned to the farm and told his master all that had happened. The story soon got round the village and nearly everyone decided to carry a piece of rowan wood in their pockets for protection. This old rhyme is a relic of this story:

> *If your whip stock's made of rowan*
> *Your nag may ride through any town.*

There were three reasons why bonfires were lit around All Hallow's Eve. One was that there was necessarily much refuse and old vegetable matter to be tidied up and burnt before the Winter, and most people just enjoyed lighting bonfires purely for this reason. Secondly people thought that by lighting fires in the open, souls condemned to Purgatory would find relief, and there are still some places in Britain that remember this custom by name. There is a field called Purgatory near Poulton in Lancashire and a farm of the same name in Weston, in the same county. The third reason for lighting bonfires was more widespread — it was done simply to scare away witches and other evil spirits. In Scotland where they celebrate this festival with much more fervour than in England, boys will go from house to house in the Aberdeen area saying, 'Give us peat to burn the witches'. It was thought that witches hovering over bonfire flames on their broomsticks would be consumed by the fire. The next day when the ashes had cooled they were scattered to fertilise the land, and everyone ran home very quickly after this, in case a witch caught up with them.

The Scottish tradition of actually burning an effigy of a witch on the Hallowe'en bonfire is, I think, only confined to that country, and has a long history. People derived much pleasure from actually seeing an effigy of the afeared witch, who represented all things evil, being burnt before their very eyes. Even in Queen Victoria's time there is a vivid account of how a hideous model of a witch riding on a trolley called a Shandy Dann was hurled onto a huge bonfire built in front of the castle at Balmoral. To the whirl of bagpipes the witch was pushed forward on her trolley and held erect by one of the company until the moment when she was thrown on the fire. This event was watched with great interest and amusement by the queen and her family.

Spells and Charms
People liked to carry torches on Hallowe'en night as the light made them feel protected against the forces of evil. These were flares made out of cabbage stalks dipped in grease or twists of dried heather or brushwood soaked in an ignitable substance. As may be seen in the next chapter, the English seemed to prefer their torch light processions on Guy Fawkes night, although some farmers on Hallowe'en carried lighted brands around their barns and granaries chanting a kind of magic spell intended to protect their stores during the Winter months. Another ritual involving a lighted torch was carried out by children. They would go into a darkened room on Hallowe'en and stand in front of a mirror holding the torch and reciting the following lines:

> *Dingle dingle dowsie, the cat's in the well,*
> *The dog's away to Berwick to buy a new bell.*

The child involved would repeat the couplet and then make a wish, while waving the torch about. The words do not seem to mean anything, but perhaps that is part of the secret of the charm.

Years ago young girls thought that they would know their future husbands if they performed certain actions. In Shropshire it was reported in the last century that six young maidens sat up until midnight in front of the fire, each with a new shift (nightdress) hanging over the back of a chair. They sat in silence until the clock struck twelve, then recited a charm which lasted ten minutes. The girl whose shift moved first after the words were said would be the next to wed.

Similarly a story from Norfolk tells us that a farmer from Morston was putting his horse away in the stable late one Hallowe'en when he noticed a light in the big barn. He crept over the yard and looked in at the window. There he saw six young labourers sitting round an upturned pitchfork, on which hung a clean shirt. They believed that the sweetheart of one of them would come and take the shirt away before midnight, if she were true to him. When nothing happened they all went home firmly convinced that none of them had a faithful girl friend.

Dreams also played an important part in fortune telling on Hallowe'en. For instance girls in Derbyshire put a crooked sixpence and a sprig of rosemary under their pillows in order to dream of future husbands. In other parts of the country a sprig of yew taken from an unknown cemetery, or nine sage leaves were used for the same purpose.

In Cornwall it was common practice to pour molten lead through the hole or handle of the front door key, into cold water, and the shape assumed by the metal would indicate the trade or profession of the future husband.

Apples were often used in fortune rituals. For instance in Nottinghamshire, among other places, pips were used when a maiden had two lovers and wanted to know which one to choose. She would take two apple pips and stick one to each cheek, after naming them for her boy friends. Next she would repeat this couplet:

> *Pippin, pippin, I thee stick thee there,*
> *That that is true thou mayst declare.*

The pip that fell off first represented the lover that she must discard.

Apple pips placed on hot coals were made use of to tell fortunes. A game that was played in Sussex consisted of everyone present taking an apple and fastening it to a string, and hanging it over a hot fire. The owner of the apple that fell first was thought to be on the point of marrying, and then the others would marry in turn as their apples fell. The last one would remain unmarried.

In Penzance, Cornwall the feast of St Just was held on Hallantide as Hallowe'en was called in that part of the country. Large Hallan apples were brought in heavy baskets to the feast and eaten together with many other delicacies. In St Ives a few miles away Hallowe'en was called Allan Day and Allan apples large and juicy were distributed to children which they did not eat immediately, but put under their pillows so that they could dream a special wish which would, they believed, come true. The fun was in the eating of the apples in bed the next morning and telling each other their dreams. There was even an Allan market where these 'fairy' apples could be bought.

Apple paring formed another fortune game. The apple was peeled carefully, so as not to break the skin, and the paring thrown over the right shoulder. Whatever letter shape it formed as it lay on the ground indicated the initial of a future lover.

Nut crack night was another name for Hallowe'en in Cheshire and the North of England years ago. Nut gathering day was important in Argyllshire, and children would go in dozens to hunt for hazel nuts to eat on Hallowe'en. The girls stitched their aprons in half so as to provide large pockets for the nuts. Fortunes were told using nuts as well as apples. A youth and a maiden would put a nut each on the fire and thinking of the loved one repeat these lines:

If he loves me pop and fly, if he hates me lie and die.

Hazel nut cakes are made in Scotland to eat on Hallowe'en.

As well as nut roasting, conker contests were held on this night in some parts of Britain. Conker contests are very old and may have developed from the egg breaking games played around Easter time. Rhymes about conker games are still repeated by children all over Britain — such as:

Hobbley hobbley onker,
My first conker,
Hobbley hobbleyho,
My first go.

Returning to Scotland, an old game called the Three Luggies was popular entertainment in the past, and Robert Burns mentions this game in his 'Hallowe'en'. Three small bowls or luggies were put on the floor or table. In one was clear water, in another foul water, and the third was left empty. The company took turns to play this game and had to be blindfolded. They were led in turn to the bowls which were switched around in between each turn, and were commanded to put their left hand into one of the bowls. If a blindfolded man chose the one with clear water, then he would marry a maiden, if it was the dirty water then he would marry a widow, and if it was the empty bowl he would remain a bachelor.

Another game pertaining to Scotland was called Hidden Charms. Charms were hidden in a dish called cream crowdie, made from fresh cream and oatmeal. The dish was passed around the company each taking a spoonful. Whoever had the ring would be the first to marry, the coin denoted wealth, the button bachelordom and the thimble a spinster. The wishbone was much sought after as it represented the heart's desire. Today mashed potatoes are used, or in more sophisticated circles a cake is baked and the charms hidden inside it.

Still in Scotland a fortune ritual called Twelve Candles used to be played on Hallowe'en. The candles were lit and set upon the floor, spaced apart, and each represented a month of the year. Beginning with Janury each contender leapt in turn over the separate candles. If at the end the candles were still all alight that meant that the participant could expect a very happy year with no misfortunes.

Hallowe'en was called Mischief Night in Yorkshire and in other parts of the country, too. Children and some adults took advantage of the fact that witches spells and curses and all manner of strange and inexplicable things were supposed to happen on this night. Children and youths took the opportunity to play tricks on citizens or people who were unpopular. Doors were unhinged, walls whitewashed, brooms and other tools left outside were taken and found in the most unlikely places — on top of the church steeple for instance! Door latches were tied, bells rung continuously. It was no joke to find that your gate had been removed and had found its way to the church yard, or that your water butt had been overturned and all the water lost.

Eventually things reached such a pass that the police intervened and prosecuted all people creating a nuisance or doing damage. Thankfully in England today Mischief Night has now virtually disappeared.

However in Scotland this kind of trickery was tolerated for much longer. Boys wearing masks called Halfins would play jokes on the locals, such as puffing smoke through letterboxes by means of lighted cabbage stalks. Or maybe they would climb onto the roof and fill the chimney top with turf, so that the smoke poured back into the house. Window tapping was a favourite pastime; the boys would tie a button onto a long piece of string and hook it over the top of the window so that the button hung down over the pane of glass. They would then stand a fair distance away and pull the string so that the button tapped the window. This would cause much concern amongst the inmates as they would open their doors to see who was tapping their windows, and find no-one there. Another trick was sham window smashing. Two lads would steal quietly up to a window, one carrying a bottle. One would tap on the window and the other would smash the bottle at the same time. Those inside would rush to the window convinced that it had been smashed. People in Scotland who complained about the pranks played upon them were made to suffer even more the next year, but those who took it all in good part were often never troubled again. It seemed that it was only fun if a trick was played on someone who was angry.

Often farmers had cabbages and turnips taken from their fields before Hallowe'en. These were used by the lads for turnip lanterns or for ammunition. The boys would happily climb onto roof tops, and hurl cabbages at the crofters when they came out to complain. Then there was a chase, which was the best part, with everyone ending up in good spirits, and the remaining vegetables were divided up amongst the poor of the village.

As it is such a magical day it is not surprising that many weather and nature customs were and are practised during Hallowe'en. For instance it was thought that in whatever way a bull faced while lying down, in that direction the wind would blow for at least three months. Farmers in Derbyshire used to go down their gardens with a lighted candle and accepted that whatever way the wind was blowing, there it would stay until Christmas.

This old rhyme from Buckinghamshire is interesting:

> *If ducks do slide at Hollantide*
> *At Christmas they will swim;*
> *If ducks do swim at Hollantide*
> *At Christmas they will slide.*

Hollantide is just another name for Hallowe'en, and the message in the rhyme simply states that if the ponds are frozen at Hallowe'en then at Christmas it will be warmer, and if it is not freezing on Hallowe'en then it will be icy at Christmas.

A curious sacrifice, obviously pagan in origin, to the sea-god Shoney used to be carried out by the inhabitants of the Isle of Lewis off the coast of Scotland. Everybody would attend church during the Autumn and bring with them a peck of malt. This was put into a large barrel and ale was brewed from it. Then one chosen from their number would wade out to sea on Hallowe'en holding a cup of ale. He would cry out, 'Shoney I give you this cup of ale, hoping that you will be so kind as to send us plenty of sea-ware for enriching our ground for the coming year'. Then he would throw the cup of ale into the sea.

The guisers of Hallowe'en seem to belong almost entirely to Scotland and the North of England. They are thought to stem directly from the Druids and are purely pagan in origin. It is thought that people dressed up on Hallowe'en as spirits, ghosts, witches, kelpies, spunkies; and blackened their faces in the bonfire ashes, as did the Druids, for protection. This is compatible with the Festival of the Dead which the Druids celebrated at this time. Some of the guisers used turnip lanterns — lamps made out of hollowed worzels or turnips, with faces cut in the sides and a lighted candle on the inside. Some say that this is also a relic of Druidism, made to represent the dead revisiting the earth for their special festival. Certainly the face lanterns give a spooky and ghost like appearance. Later the guisers became more civilised and dressed more elegantly, going from house to house entertaining with plays and concerts in return for a meal and money. Guising in this manner became very popular over a hundred years ago, and provided entertainment similar to the mummers' plays. Nowadays the children do the guising and have reverted back to the old traditions of dressing as witches, goblins, etc.

Turnips lanterns are known in other parts of the country. In Norfolk, for instance, at Hallowe'en, and in Somerset in the little village of Hinton St George there is a festival of 'punkies' as they are called in that part of the world. The Hinton St George lanterns can be traced back to 1840. Apparently the women of the village were worried that their menfolk had not returned from their work on Hallowe'en. It was becoming dark and the men had taken the lanterns. One of the women had the idea of making rough lanterns out of hollowed out turnips. The others followed her lead, and soon they had made up a search party lit with the home made lanterns to look for the menfolk of the village. After that it became a tradition in the village to make these punkies every Hallowe'en, and the idea spread. Some wonderful creations were made, with intricate designs, pictures and patterns being cut out of the sides of the turnips. Today there is still a punkie festival at Hinton St George and there is a competition for the best made lantern. This rhyme is chanted as the children march with their punkies around the village:

> *It's punkie night tonight,*
> *It's punkie night tonight,*
> *Give us a candle, give us a light,*
> *It's punkie night tonight.*

Other festivities as well as the punkie competition in this small village include eating, concerts and dancing. It is not known why the lanterns are called punkies. The Scottish name for a water sprite is a Spunkie, and in America these type of lanterns are made out of pumpkins and are called punkies. Perhaps the name is a combination of both.

Games
Apart from dressing up and performing concerts or charades like the children do in Scotland when they go guising, there are a few traditional games which people like to play on Hallowe'en — especially if you have a party.

First Bob Apple or Apple Dooking as they call it in Scotland. For this you need a fairly large tub or bowl half filled with water and set in the middle of the floor. Put in about a dozen apples, and the idea of the game is to catch an apple in your mouth, keeping your hands behind your back. This causes quite a bit of fun, because you have no idea how slippery the apple can be, or how hard it is to get a grip on it with your teeth. And of course you can get very wet doing it. Every member of the party has a turn and a set time allotted then they have to wait until their turn comes round again, and the game goes on until all the apples are eaten.

Snap Apple is another game which can be played. Apples are attached to string and hung from a beam or from the ceiling. The same principle applies as in Bob Apple and the apple can only be caught with the teeth, and not touched by any other part of the body.

Hanch Apple was popular with adults years ago but is too dangerous for children to try. A horizontal rod was suspended from the ceiling and an apple fixed at one end and a lighted candle at the other. The competitor had to bite the apple with his hands tied behind his back at the same time avoiding the lighted candle which always seemed to swing in his direction at the wrong moment.

HALLOWE'EN CUSTOMS
Apples make lovely dishes and in Scotland no Hallowe'en supper is complete without the apple pie or the toffee apples. In England in some northern parts the day was known as Cake Day because of a tradition that the woman of the house would bake a cake for each member of the family according to his or her taste. Hallowe'en cakes are nowadays decorated with witches, cats, broomsticks or other items which are linked with this festival.

Recipes
Here is a simple recipe for *toffee apples* which are eaten in Scotland every Hallowe'en. Children like them and should be encouraged to make them.

Ingredients:

4 or 5 washed apples	4 or 5 wooden skewers
½ lb (220 g) sugar)	

Method. Make a caramel by sifting the sugar through a fine sieve, and melting it in a shallow pan over a moderate heat. Stir all the time to prevent the sugar from sticking or burning. When the liquid is coffee coloured it is ready for the apples to be dipped in one by one after each has been pierced with a skewer. Turn the apples round carefully until the whole surface has been covered with the toffee. Then lay the apples on buttered paper to harden.

As mentioned it was the tradition in the North of England to make a different sort of *cake* for each member of the family on Hallowe'en. Each bun had a different flavour or filling and they were eaten with a wish at teatime. They were thought to have magical powers to grant wishes years ago.

Ingredients: (to make six or eight buns)

2 oz (50 g) butter or margarine
2 oz (50 g) sugar
2 oz (50 g) flour (self-raising)
1 large egg
various flavourings in small
quantities such as ½ teaspoon
coffee, cocoa, or dessicated
coconut or caraway seeds

1 teaspoonful currants or
sultanas or chopped nuts or
chopped glace cherries
6 or 8 paper bun cases

Method. Light the oven at Regulo mark 6 or 400 F. Cream the butter and sugar together until light and fluffy. Beat the egg and then add to the mixture, add the flour and if necessary a teaspoonful of milk. Take five small basins and divide the mixture equally between them not forgetting an equal amount to be left in the large bowl for a plain one. Mix a different flavour into each small bowl, and transfer into the bun cases. Put the cases on a baking tray and cook in oven until golden brown —usually for about ten minutes. Cut out witch shapes on broomsticks and stick them onto the top of the buns when cold. Or another idea is to put a small lucky charm into each bun wrapped in greaseproof paper like they did 'north of the border' years ago.

Another delicious recipe coming from Scotland for Hallowe'en is for *Hazel nut biscuits.*

Ingredients:

8 oz (220 g) flour
6 oz (150 g) chopped hazel nuts,
    or walnuts would do
12 oz (375 g) castor sugar

3 oz (75 g) butter
1 egg
1 egg yolk
teaspoonful of water

Method. Melt the butter and let it cool. Add chopped nuts to egg and sugar and mix well, and then stir in the flour. Lastly stir in the cooled butter. Roll the dough onto a floured board until about ¾ inch (2 cms) thick. Cut into rounds with cutter. Make a tiny slit on top of each biscuit and paint surface with egg yolk and water mixed. Bake for about 20 minutes at Regulo mark 2 or at 300F. There should be about 20 biscuits.

Things For Children To Make:

To make a *turnip lantern* you will need:

a good size turnip or pumpkin
a candle
pieces of lolly sticks, paper and
  crayons, and a cocktail stick
crepe paper cut to make hair,
  cotton wool for beard and
  moustache

piece of string or cord for
  handle
long pin or nail
glue and a piece of carrot for
  nose

First slice off the top of the turnip but do not throw away. Next scoop out the flesh from inside, being careful not to break the skin at any point. If children are doubtful about doing this, they should ask an adult to help them. When a fair size hollow has been made then concentrate on cutting the face from the outside. Cut the mouth shape and the eyes big enough to let the candle light shine through clearly. A nose could be cut out of a piece of carrot and stuck onto the face with a cocktail stick. Hair may be cut out of crepe paper and stuck on for good effect, and ears made and coloured out of stiff paper and stuck or pinned on the sides of the face. A beard or moustache made out of coloured cotton wool might be fixed in the right places by glue. Two holes pierced on each side of the face could be used to thread the cord for the handle. Next place the candle upright at the bottom of the inside of the lantern, and fix into position with a pin or nail pushed through from the bottom of the outside of the turnip into the base of the candle. The top piece of the turnip can either be decorated with hair or left bald. Light the candle, replace the top, fixing with a little sticky tape.

Children would enjoy holding a Hallowe'en party where their guests brought their 'punkies' with them. The turnip lanterns could be placed on the tea tables and lit in an otherwise darkened room. They could parade around the garden after dark with their

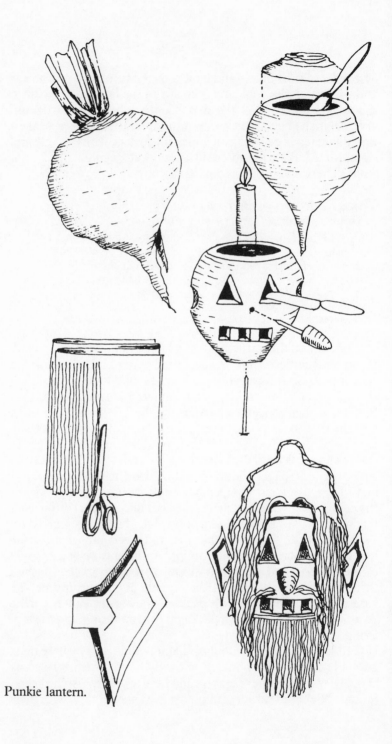

Punkie lantern.

lighted lanterns to increase the fun. Competitions might be held to judge the best efforts.

Witches' hats and Goblin ears are fun to make. In the Scottish tradition of guising, children might dress up as witches, ghosts or goblins for a Hallowe'en party.

For the *witch hat* all that is needed is:

a circle of black paper approximately 18 inches (45 cms) in diameter
a long piece of black paper approximately 6 inches (15 cms) wide — the length depending on the size of the head for the brim
glue and sticky tape
gold and silver paper for cut-outs

Mark the centre of the circle of black paper and draw a line from the middle to the outside edge. Cut along this line and then overlap the paper until the hat is in the shape of a dunce's cap. Fit the shape to the head and when the right size glue the edges of the hat together. To make the brim cut inch deep cuts along one side of the piece of long black paper. Paste the line of inscissions and tuck round the edge of the hat sticking the cut pieces inside. Fold the brim into shape. Cut out various Hallowe'en shapes such as witches, cats, new moons and so on and stick on the front of the hat.

The boys might like to make *Goblin ears*. All that is needed is:

a piece of cardboard 12x8 inches (30 x 20 cms)
a piece of hat elastic
crayons and a black pen

Divide the cardboard into two and draw an ear shape. Cut out and use as a template making another identical ear. Colour both sides of the ear and add ear lines with a black pen. Punch two holes in each cardboard ear and thread elastic through and tie in a loop. The 'ears' can then be looped over normal ears.

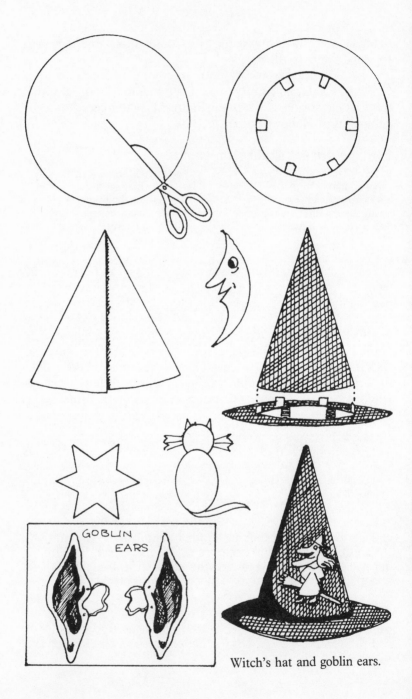

Witch's hat and goblin ears.

GUY FAWKES DAY — 5 NOVEMBER

When Queen Elizabeth I died James VI of Scotland, the son of Mary Queen of Scots, inherited the throne and became James I of England. We all know the general story of Guy Fawkes and his friends and how they conspired to blow up the Houses of Parliament, but I wonder if many people know the reason why these people came to plan such a drastic deed.

It all started long before Guy Fawkes was born, when the hatred between Protestants and Catholics grew to alarming proportions. It was Henry VIII who broke away from the Catholic faith and the power of the Pope and created the Protestant church in Britain. From that time onwards people suffered for their religion depending on the faith of the ruling monarch. When a Protestant was in power the Catholics had a very hard time of it, and when a Catholic monarch reigned then the Protestants suffered greatly.

Guy Fawkes was born in York and the site of his house can still be seen. He was the son of a wealthy lawyer, and his mother, too, had money of her own. The Fawkes were Protestants but many of their friends were Catholics and were entertained by the Fawkes family.

After his father's death Guy inherited much of the estate although he was still quite young. He became more and more interested in the Catholic faith, and finally decided to become a member of that religion.

As soon as he was able he joined the Spanish army and was sent on his own request to fight in Belgium, against the Dutch. It may appear strange that an Englishman should fight for another country, but Guy Fawkes was now an ardent Catholic, and Spain hoped that one day Britain would belong to the Spanish empire. The King of Spain was friendly towards English Catholics and hoped that they would overthrow the government and in so doing give Spain the opportunity of taking over the country.

Fawkes was a good soldier and was given the rank of Colonel although only in his twenties. He looked after his troops well and organised the fighting so as to avoid unnecessary loss of life. He was also an expert on the use of gunpowder, and in those days very few people knew much about this 'dangerous stuff', except that it had to be handled and stored with care.

Colonel Fawkes had no part in the planning of the gunpowder plot. That daring idea was devised by Catholics back in England, who had grown desperate at the way they were being treated. They had hoped that the new king, although a Protestant would be lenient and let the Catholics live in peace, but this was not to be. Although James himself did not want to harm the Catholics his ministers put pressure on him to pass harsh laws penalising members of this religion. They feared a Catholic uprising which might succeed in removing the king from the throne and substituting a Catholic monarch. This was the origin of the gunpowder plot. If the ministers of the crown had let the Catholics live in peace, then there would have been no need for any kind of plot to overthrow the king and Parliament.

Robert Catesby is generally considered to be the originator of the plot. He was at one time Protestant but turned Catholic, as Fawkes did, when a young man. He devised a plan that would put an end to the persecution of the Catholics 'with one blow'. Thomas Wintour and his brother were the next to be involved, and then Guy Fawkes was asked if he would be willing to take part. Catesby impressed on Fawkes how important it was that they had a man who was well versed in the properties of gunpowder, and Fawkes was so impressed and honoured at being asked to take on such an important task that he readily agreed without much thought of the consequences.

More and more people became involved in the plan, and, Thomas Percy, who was one of the king's courtiers managed to rent a house next door to the Houses of Parliament without arousing any suspicion. The idea was to tunnel through the wall of the house into the Parliament building itself and secrete the barrels of gunpowder and combustible fuel needed to make the explosion effective, in through the hole in the wall. The rooms were on street level, and not in cellars as we have been led to believe, and the actual state chambers where the ministers and the king sat were on the first floor of the Parliament building.

The conspirators arranged for many provisions to be brought into the house so that they need not arouse the suspicions of neighbours, by going in and out to fetch food. The walls of the house proved very thick, and the plotters, all men of noble birth, and not used to hard labour, found the task of tunnelling through very tiring and frustrating indeed. One day they heard the tolling of a bell deep down under the spot where they were tunnelling, and the sound frightened them so much that they sprinkled holy water on the place to avert evil superstition and the curse of the devil.

Another time a loud rumbling noise seemed to come from the room to which they were trying to gain access, and all were pitifully afraid that the whole place was going to collapse about their ears. It was Guy Fawkes, himself, who assured them that it was only a coal merchant removing his coal from one room to another. The merchant was approached and admitted that he owned the room which lay directly underneath the State Chamber of Parliament. He agreed to let the conspirators rent the room for a short length of time. Here was a bit of luck, and the plotters thankfully threw down their shovels and pick axes, and moved into the coveted room. It was a simple matter to bring from a house across the river under the cover of darkness, the barrels of gunpowder, iron bars, wood faggots and sacks to cover and keep dry the explosive powder.

The opening of Parliament was fixed for 31 October, but the king postponed the occasion because he wanted to attend a hunting party at Royston, and so 5 November was agreed upon for the opening date. The conspirators were rather worried by this alteration to their plans, and Guy Fawkes became increasingly worried about the state of the gunpowder. It was very damp and misty by the river; and in fact, even if the fuses had been lit it is quite possible that the gunpowder would have been too wet to have caused any kind of explosion.

It was planned to kill James and his elder son Prince Henry who would be at the opening of Parliament, and also of course all the ministers of the crown. It was natural therefore that arguments broke out within the group of plotters, because many had friends and relatives in Parliament, and did not wish them to be killed too. So on 26 October a letter was sent to a Catholic peer, Lord Mounteagle, telling him not to be present at the opening of Parliament on 5 November. The sender is thought by some to be Francies Tresham, one of the conspirators, who was the brother-in-law of Lord Mounteagle. In the note were these words: 'Though there be no appearance of any stir, yet I say they shall receive a terrible blow, the Parliament, and yet they shall not see who hurts them'.

The plan was that when all the peers and the kings had assembled, Guy Fawkes would light the fuse, which was a trail of gunpowder, leading to the barrels with a slow burning match, or flare, and then make his escape to Flanders before the explosion, aboard a boat that would be waiting for him on the river alongside the building.

The king was not told of the letter immediately as he was on a hunting trip, and so Lord Mounteagle and the Lord Chamberlain decided to search the rooms beneath the Chamber of State, and of course Guy Fawkes was discovered. He pretended to be doing a job for Thomas Percy, who owned the building next door. The two officials looked around but did not let Fawkes know that they suspected anything.

Meanwhile, as part of the plot, a man called Everad Digby agreed to assemble his Catholic allies on Dunsmore Heath in Warwickshire as if for a hunting party. When news that the plan had been carried out successfully reached them, then the revolution would start. Prince Charles, the second son of King James would be placed on the throne, and as he was still a child he would be in the hands of his ministers and therefore would do what he was told. In case Prince Charles escaped plans were laid to seize Princess Elizabeth, sister of the two princes, and to put her on the throne if necessary.

On the morning of 5 November at two o'clock a party of soldiers under the magistrate Sir Thomas Knevett went to the room where Guy Fawkes was hiding with the explosives. He was arrested and taken to Whitehall Palace where he was interrogated by James and his councillors. James had previously read the warning letter, and having a horror of gunpowder — his own father Lord Darnley had been killed by it years before — was convinced that this is what was meant in the letter, and of course he was right.

Other conspirators were overtaken fleeing the city, and Fawkes and seven others were taken to the Tower. There they were questioned and tortured to reveal the names of the others in the plot. Fawkes was a brave man and gave nothing away. After the trial he and his companions were found guilty of treason and were executed on 31 January 1606, opposite the building they had planned to blow up. The prisoners were hung drawn and quartered as was the practice then.

Robert Catesby, the ring leader, and others engaged in a dramatic gun battle at the mansion of Holbeach. Catesby and some of his followers were shot and the rest taken prisoner.

There were many in the gunpowder plot that were never found out, but legend has it that two Jesuit priests, Father Garnett and Father Hall, who were participants in the plot, went into hiding in a mansion called Hendlip Hall about four miles from Worcester. The large rambling house owned by Mr and Mrs Abingdon was renowned for its secret rooms, cavities, vaults and passages. Staircases were concealed in walls, retreats up chimneys and trapdoors abounded in the most unlikely places. The house was situated on a hill and therefore its inmates could keep a look out for approaching strangers. During the first few weeks after the failure of the plot a servant of Catesby's confessed that Father Garnett was involved in the plot, and Hendlip Hall being known for its secret hiding places was at once visited by Sir Henry Bromley and his men, who had been appointed by the government to find the fugitive. He was told to look for suspiciously thick walls, unusually shaped rooms and fireplaces, and to listen for any unaccountable noises. After searching for four days two men were found in a vault half dead with hunger, but they were not Jesuits. The officials were just about to leave when another confession by a tortured conspirator in the Tower revealed that another Jesuit priest was hiding at Hendlip. The Abingdons denied all knowledge of this, but after another ten days search both Garnett and Hall gave themselves up — from lack of air rather than food. They had hidden in a small space between two chimneys backing onto one another, and had been fed through a small hole in the chimney wall by a reed from a gentlewoman's chamber. They had been fed on honey, jam and sweet liquids. They were in great pain for their limbs had swollen up owing to the cramped conditions of the hiding place, and they had no room to move. Garnett said afterwards that if the place had been cleared of furniture and books which took up much valuable space and air, then they could have existed there for as long as three months. (This account is taken from Jardine's Narrative of the Gunpowder Plot 1857.)

Here is a part of a poem entitled 'Song on the Fifth of November' and it may well have been attributed to a Jesuit priest:

> *There's a plot to beguile*
> *An obstinate isle.*
> *Great Britain that heretic nation.*
> *Why so slyly behav'd*
> *In the hopes to be saved*
> *By the help of the curs'd reformation.*
>
> *There's powder enough*
> *And combustible stuff*
> *In thirty and odd trusty barrels,*
> *We'll send them together*
> *The Lord can tell whither*
> *And decide at one blow all their quarrels.*
>
> *When the King and his son*
> *And the parliament's gone*
> *And the people are left in the lurch*
> *Things will take their old station*
> *In the curs'd nation —*
> *And I'll be the head of the Church.*

It is interesting to note that the Palace of Westminster which housed the House of Lords chamber on the first floor was a vaulted stone building dating back to the thirteenth century. As mentioned earlier, the 'cellar' in which Fawkes hid the explosive was in reality at street level. But as the room was vaulted like a cellar people began to be confused about it, and over the centuries believed that the famous vaults were underground. In 1834 a great tally stick fire did what the plotters failed to do over two hundred years previously — namely destroyed the Houses of Parliament completely. The building was later erected 40 feet to the east of the original designed by Sir Charles Barry. Therefore the site of the Gunpowder Plot today is no more than an open space in the centre of the State Officer Court, an area used for dumping waste metal, and which houses an emergency generator.

The 'vaults' are nowadays searched ceremoniously by an officer and ten men of the Yeomen of the Guard wearing their traditional uniforms, and carrying a lantern. During the last war the duty was carried out by a company of the Home Guard. The search only covers the ground where the Houses of Parliament used to be and is purely formal. Other more modern methods are employed to enforce security inside the building used today.

A small collection of books and illustrations relating to the Gunpowder Plot and donated by Messrs Catesby can be seen in the Record Office of the House of Lords.

Many rhymes about Guy Fawkes have survived over the centuries and in some he is described as carrying a 'dark' lantern. There is an old lantern on display in the Ashmolean Museum, Oxford and it is believed to have been the original lantern used by the conspirator himself. Justice Heywood, one of the Justices of the Peace who arrested Fawkes, kept the lantern after the trial, and when he died his son Robert Heywood took possession of it. Robert Heywood had been a proctor of Brasenose College, Oxford since 1639, and in 1641 he gave the lantern to the Bodleian Museum also in Oxford. In 1887 the lantern was transferred to the Ashmolean Museum where it can be seen today. The lantern is desicribed as being about 11 inches high, made of iron, which is very rusty now, with a candle holder inside. The top consists of an inverted fluted funnel and there is a handle attached to the cylinder. It originally contained glass but that has long since disappeared. The lantern was made dark by the closing of a shutter which consisted of a hinged door frame containing dark glass. When the shutter was closed only a limited amount of light was released, and that was why it was called a 'dark' lantern.

At Rushton Hall before 1830 another lantern believed to be the original owned by Guy Fawkes could be seen. It was described by a writer of the time as a fine piece of workmanship both in secrecy and ornament, possessing at the bottom a mechanical device by which the candle could be crushed in the hand at a moment's notice. It turned with speed and could be rendered a 'dark' lantern in a split second. It also had a strong reflector and bore traces of gilt with which it was once decorated.

Unfortunately since the time of writing this lantern has been lost without trace.

Bonfires

Old rhymes often reveal the customs associated with festivals. Guy Fawkes Day has far the most rhymes connected with it, known both nationally and locally, than any of the other festivals mentioned in this book. Although I have written about the origins of rhymes in my book *Origins of Rhymes, Songs and Sayings,* I think it is only appropriate to repeat some of the Bonfire night verses in this section. They seem to fall into three groups. Those which describe the plot itself, for example 'Remember, remember the Fifth of November'. The collecting rhymes which children chanted when begging for fuel for the bonfire:

> *We want a faggot to make it alight*
> *Hatches and duckets, beetles and wedges*
> *If you don't give us some, we'll pull down your old hedges.*

And the chants and prayers sung around the bonfire:

> *Rumour, rumour, pump and derry,*
> *Prick his heart and burn his body,*
> *And send his soul to Purgatory.*

As early as 1607 we have a record of Bonfire celebrations at Bristol on 5 November. James I had declared the day a public holiday in his joy at the overthrow of the Gunpowder Plot. Bonfires played an important part in the early celebrations, perhaps more so than they do today. As mentioned in the chapter on Hallowe'en people had lit bonfires around this time of year since pagan times, to ward off evil forces which were thought to approach the world with the coming of Winter and the long dark nights. There are many rituals associated with bonfires and many of them were continued throughout the centuries on 5 November.

The Lucky Stones game was a favourite with children of long ago. They would hunt for a stone of a peculiar shape or colour or size or maybe one with a hole in it, with a striped or ridged pattern. When the 'lucky stones' had been chosen the children would wait until the celebrations were nearly over, and then throw stones into the red ashes of the bonfire, recite a rhyme or charm, and the next morning when the ashes were cold they would hunt for their individual stones. If the stones were unbroken and not discoloured it promised a year of happiness and good luck for the owners. If on the other hand the stones were found to be broken or burnt then ill fortune would follow for the children concerned.

Children would often black their faces with the ashes on Bonfire night, in imitation of Guy Fawkes who it was believed did this to try and camouflage himself.

Bonfires were often lit in the middle of towns in the past, in spite of the fact that the wooden houses were very much at risk. Old customs die hard, and it was perhaps centuries before new bonfire sites could be decided on. For example a large bonfire was always lit in the Cathedral yard at Exeter, the Cornhill in Bridgwater, and in many densely populated places in Birming-ham and London. In London a huge bonfire was traditionally built and lit in Lincoln's Inn Fields. It consisted of about two hundred cartloads of fuel, and 30 guys. Marvellous firework displays were also organised, and these will be dealt with later.

Bonfires in the past have played another more practical part in our history. Before the telephone or telegram they were the only quick way, beside the ringing of bells, to warn people across the country of approaching danger. In times of war, expected invasions or plague, beacons were always at the ready to be lit on cliff and hill tops at a moment's notice. Men known as the beacon men tended these warning posts and they became professional fire lighters. It is thought by some that these men were employed in building bonfires for 5 November celebrations. Helped by their enthusiasm and proficiency, the passion for making bonfires spread to all parts of the country and the tradition of fires, tar barrels, guys and fireworks grew and has remained unbroken except for wartime, for nearly four hundred years.

As mentioned bells, too, were widely used in early times to spread messages of good or bad tidings. When the news of the safe deliverance of James I and his ministers from the most daring plot in our history reached loyal subjects all over Britain, church bells began to peal out the good tidings with a fervour unknown in British history. The number of bells rung on Guy Fawkes Day far exceeded the bells rung on Shrove Tuesday or at Christmas time. They continued with joyful peals throughout the day and it is not surprising that Guy Fawkes Day was often known as Ringing Day.

The anti-Catholic feeling was naturally very strong in earlier times, not only because of the nature of the plot, but because many people had suffered for their faith in the previous century. In fact in Lewes, Sussex 17 martyrs were burnt at the stake some 50 years previous to the Plot, and the inhabitants never forgot the incident. The Protestants wanted to keep the anti-Catholic feeling alive and during the reign of Charles II the Green Ribbon club was formed in London to whip up fervour against the Catholics on 5 November. In 1688 William of Orange who was to become William III of England landed on British soil on Guy Fawkes Day. Some say that this was deliberate to remind people of the Plot, and the occasion was celebrated by the Protestants by the formation of the Orange Institution which aimed at protecting Protestants but condemning Catholics.

Apart from the religious feeling there was a much more practical reason why this day remained so popular with the common folk. For this was the holiday when they could air their grievances without fear of being punished. The starvation wages of the farm workers, the inhuman conditions imposed on factory workers during the industrial revolution and after, and the suppression of the poor in general, resulted in vandalism, looting, damaging of property and general bad behaviour on 5 November. The poor used the public holiday to show their discontent with their meagre lot in a very positive way. Shopkeepers and owners of other property boarded up their windows and doors for protection against wilful damage and fire.

Gangs of bonfire boys roamed the streets tearing down fences and taking anything combustible for the bonfires. Although the civic authorities did their best to organise activities so that they were carried out in a civilised way, the gangs nearly always managed to turn the celebration into a riot. Tar barrels were set alight and rolled willy nilly from high ground into holiday crowds, and so into danger areas such as houses and shops. The people thought this great fun and ignored the danger. They screamed with laughter as they jumped out of the way of a blazing tar barrel as it careered down the hill, and then followed it to kick it to pieces when it came to rest.

The Guys

It is not certain when guys were first introduced to the proceedings and in some places they were not thought essential items for 5 November. In other places they were regarded as most important; in Exeter, Hereford, Worcester, Bridgwater, Lewes and London, to name but a few. It seems strange that although James I was James VI of Scotland before becoming King of England, that the Scots do not celebrate the failure of the Gunpowder Plot — in fact to this day it is hardly known in Scotland. On the other hand the Scots make much more of Hallowe'en and it was usual to burn effigies of witches on bonfires on 31 October. Here seems the real link as to why guys became so popular in England. It was probably James and his Scottish ministers, well versed in the Hallowe'en witch burning tradition who introduced the idea of burning an effigy of the hated Guy Fawkes on celebration bonfires. Besides, the burning of enemy effigies goes back to the dark ages and is truly a pagan practice. In Mexico and other parts of the world it has been the custom to burn a model of Judas, the man who betrayed Jesus, on certain saint days. Also in France there is a story of a soldier who stabbed the statue of the Virgin Mary in a fit of temper, and was consequently lynched by the mob. His effigy was burnt for many years after this to commemorate the event. So it is not surprising that models of the infamous Guy Fawkes were soon burnt on 5 November in the reign of James I.

The guys in the former days were fashioned very similarly to the ones made today. A stuffed head with a mask and a tall seventeenth century styled hat complete with paper ribbons, a body shaped and stuffed with straw and arms and legs made from pieces of wood, and dressed in coat, trousers and sometimes a waistcoat. The colours in those days were usually grey or brown, and the figure was seen holding the traditional 'dark' lantern. A record of an extremely large guy has been found which was burnt during the reign of Charles II in London. The effigy was made with real live cats inside his body that squealed realistically when the bonfire was lit, much to the satisfaction of the crowd. (I hope that the cats escaped before they were overcome by smoke.)

Later children made guys a few days before the event and paraded the streets chanting, 'a penny for the guy', sometimes pushing the model in an old pram or leaning it up against the wall at street corners. In some places such as Ramsgate and Cambridge the boys themselves dressed up as guys and went from street to street begging for pennies.

In other towns small doll guys were made usually by the girls, who showed their handiwork in a box cradle before collecting money.

Other enemies of the country were burnt on 5 November, and the Pope was probably the most popular one years ago. The feeling against Catholicism was very strong and it was well into the present century before places like Lewes in Sussex would tolerate a Catholic church in the vicinity. Models of Napoleon were burnt during the Napoleonic wars, the Czar during the Crimean war, the Kaiser during the First World War, and of course Adolf Hitler during the last war. Since that time we seem to have reverted back to Guy Fawkes. A rhyme chanted by the children of Derbyshire during the Crimean war reminds us that the Battle of Inkerman was fought successfully for us on 5 November in 1854:

> *Remember, remember the Fifth of November,*
> *Inkerman, powder and shot,*
> *When General Liprandi attacked John, Pat and Sandy,*
> *And a jolly good licking he got.*

John, Pat and Sandy represented the English, Irish and Scottish soldiers fighting in the campaign.

An amusing 'guy' story which occurred in 1825, just before 5 November, tells of how a poor man was eating his meagre breakfast in his small attic or garret before going to work when a meassage came to him that someone wanted to see him in the street. Being curious he went down and was met by three or four youths. Before he realised what was happening he was forced to sit in a chair and his arms and legs were tied to it. Then he was dressed as a guy and his face painted, and a lantern and matches attached to his hands to make him appear more life-like! He was paraded all day through the streets while his captors collected money for their 'guy'. It was not until late evening that he was finally released and allowed home. The next day the man went and complained to the local police at the station near his home. Consequently the offenders were brought before the magistrate and fined or put into prison. The judge ruled that it is illegal to 'smug' a man for a 'guy'.

Food for Bonfire night

As well as burning guys the bonfires were used to cook potatoes on this special night, and this custom can be traced back many years. For weeks, large potatoes — 'roasters' as they were called in Derbyshire were stored in readiness for 'Bunfireneet'. Some potatoes weighed as much as half a pound and there was nothing nicer or so the locals thought, than eating a hot floury roaster with just a 'pinch o' sawt', with the glow of the bonfire on your face and the merry jests and chants of the party around you.

Treacle toffee was made in Yorkshire years ago for children to chew while enjoying themselves around the bonfire. An old Yorkshire rhyme tells us that an old woman from Cleasby made and sold this sweetmeat called 'Tomtrot' on 5 November.

'Gunpowder Plot shall never be forget, as long as Bella Brown sells Tomtrot'.

Also in the north other foods associated with Bonfire night were Parkin and Thor cakes. Parkin, a kind of oatmeal and treacle cake was so widely eaten on this festival that in some parts of Yorkshire it was called Parkin Day. Like so many other customs the making of Parkin can be traced back to pagan times. It was originally made to welcome the dead back to earth on All Hallows or All Souls day namely the 1 November. It was commonly thought as I explained in the Hallowe'en section that this was the time that the dead visited their families. In Yorkshire, Parkin was baked as a special dish to welcome the dead. When people became more civilised they gave up this rather weird custom and honoured their dead in churchyards with ornamental grave stones and flowers. But along came Guy Fawkes and the custom of making Parkin took on a new meaning, was put back a few days, and is now as popular as ever.

Thor or Thar cakes widely made and eaten in Derbyshire and

Lancashire on 5 November also had their origins in pagan mythology. It is thought that these cakes, made out of oatmeal, treacle and peel were eaten in honour of the feast day of the Scandinavian god Thor. It was the custom years ago for children to save up money and ingredients to make Thor cakes and the feast was called 'Thar cake joining'. People took turns each year to hold celebrations in their respective houses. The question 'Have you joined yet?' before 5 November — meant 'Have you made your Thar cakes yet?' Some clubs and churches in the north still hold Thar cake suppers on the nearest Saturday to 5 November.

Fireworks
It was the Chinese who first invented fireworks or pyrotechnics which is the technical name for them. A firework consists of a case usually made out of paper or cardboard to form a tube, and filled with a special explosive mixture. Although the case may be completely sealed, when the mixture is ignited it will burn continuously giving off a force of gas until it is burnt away. Usually the flame will not burn without oxygen but in the case of the firework one of the ingredients is salt petre (potassium nitrate) and this chemical gives off oxygen when ignited. This salt is found in abundance throughout the East and it was here that firework powder consisting of salt petre, sulphur and charcoal was first used.

Fireworks were made in China long before the birth of Christ and it was the Chinese who first invented the rocket to be used in wartime as well as a peace time entertainment. In Arabia, too, we know that the Moslem alchemists developed the range of fireworks in the seventh century, but it was not until the thirteenth century that the knowledge of this art reached Europe and the first European country to produce them was Italy. The gun was invented in the fourteenth century and the explosive firework powder was adapted to suit its needs, and that is how gunpowder got its name.

Pyrotechnics usually fall into two groups. Those producing flame and those producing sparks and movement using greater force. The flame fireworks have thin cases that burn away with the ingredients. This group includes coloured lights of all kinds, Roman candles and stars sent out by rocket shells. The cases of the second type are stronger and do not burn with the contents. The pressure set up by gases resulting from the mixture burning inside the case throws out a jet of partly consumed particles or sparks to give the golden rain effect. Ingredients such as iron or steel filings, lamp black or charcoal give varying effects. The internal pressure of the burning gases is especially strong in the rocket and the Catherine wheel and this is what propels the rocket into the sky, and turns the Catherine wheel round with such force.

Until the beginning of the nineteenth century the only colours seen in fireworks were the ordinary flame colours of red, orange and yellow. Then the chemical called potassium chlorate was introduced to the mixture which then burnt with sufficient heat to turn metal to gas thus tinting the flame. Barium salts give a green flame, strontium, red, sodium, yellow and copper with chlorine gas gives a blue light.

During the Middle Ages and after, firework displays were in great demand at most religious festivals in Europe, and later became a feature at most public rejoicings such as the ending of a war or the crowning of a new monarch. These displays were handled by experts, military fireworkers, who were responsible for explosives during wartime. In peacetime they were in great demand, and it is quite possible tht Guy Fawkes himself was a military fireworker when not engaged on active service. The firework experts were responsible for making their own fireworks and for designing continuous displays and set pieces that would enthrall the public. Marvellous firework pictures were created which were true works of art. Even before Guy Fawkes firework displays in the previous century were in great demand, and it is known that they were one of Queen Elizabeth I's favourite forms of entertainment. At first only foreign designers were employed but gradually a few British learnt from the continent the intricate art of pyrotechnics.

Pleasure gardens sprang up over the years advertising marvellous displays of fireworks, the most outstanding being the one at Vauxhall Gardens in London. Later this was superceded by the famous Crystal Palace spectacular staged by C. T. Brock, the man who developed the firework for commercial use in Britain over the last hundred years. The Crystal Palace displays lasted from 1865 to 1936 when the building was burnt down.

Large firework displays were often given alongside a great expanse of water. The effect was doubly increased by the reflection on the water's surface. In London, for instance, years ago barges were used, bearing set pieces, which floated down the river Thames, thus giving the crowds a good chance to see the spectacle, from both sides of the river. Flares were attached to small floats or buoys and glowed for quite a long time on the water surface. The most spectacular of all was the sight of the underwater fireworks which dipped and dived and seemed to keep alight under water as well as in the air. These were often called water rockets or skimmers.

Bridges, too, were often used to anchor the frame of a large set piece or firework picture which when lit would provide a strong background and prevent the frame from collapsing too soon and falling into the water before the picture had burnt right through. The only danger was to the houses and other buildings which were present in previous centuries on the bridge, as a spark could set alight the whole street.

In the eighteenth century water firework displays were at the height of their popularity especially on 5 November. George III and his family watched the events from a specially constructed royal box built on one of the banks of the river Thames. The watermen lent their barges for the occasion and elaborate pictures were displayed. Among the more memorable were St Paul's Cathedral, the Tower of London, portraits of the king and his family, and of course pictures of Guy Fawkes himself complete with lantern and gunpowder barrels.

It is generally agreed that the rocket and the fountain are the two oldest types of fireworks, the fountain being just a simple flare, and the rocket developed as previously stated. The Roman candle with its reputation for spasmodic flame is thought to have a long history also. Legend has it that a carnival held in Rome before Lent, centuries ago, consisted of people parading the streets holding lighted candles. The aim of the people in the parade seemed to be to extinguish other candles while keeping their own alight. This continuous lighting and putting out of flames probably gave the firework its name — so the Roman candle is in reality just a development of the ordinary household candle.

Squibs were made from rolls of paper, folded with gunpowder

inside. It is known that miners used them for centuries to blast rock surfaces, and they were also used to a lesser degree in homes to dislodge soot from chimneys. Miners did a good trade in home made squibs on Bonfire night until about 50 years ago. The Catherine wheel is not thought to be very old, less than two hundred years, in fact. This firework, sometimes known as the pinwheel has become as popular as the rocket and is made to the same formula, the only difference being that the case burns away with the ingredients.

But perhaps the most popular firework of all is still the jumping jack or grasshopper. The banging jumping effect is obtained by crushing the powder inside the case to such an extent that the firework goes off spasmodically with a bang. This creation can be claimed to be entirely British and now the principle is applied to the tails of rockets to make them bang and jump in the sky.

Torches and flares were popular with ordinary people. They felt safe holding a cabbage stalk dipped in grease and lighted at one end, and enjoyed parading around their village or town in a torchlight procession on Bonfire night. In fact, after the failure of the Gunpowder Plot the common people felt the urge to join in proceedings and take an active part in the celebrations themselves — not just be content with being the audience watching set displays.

Small towns and villages across Britain could not afford the services of a professional military fireworker, and so set about making their own displays, and their own fireworks. In back rooms, shops and even bakeries, fireworks were made to well guarded formulas, each village or neighbour trying to outdo the next. In many places in the west country and the south coast such achievements became very popular. Bridgwater became famous for its giant squibs and Lewes for its 'rousers'.

Firework factories became established during the last century, partly as a result of commercial enterprise, and partly so that they could be made under regulated conditions with due care and attention. Surprisingly though, even today, most fireworks are still produced by hand in factories. Shops began to sell factory made fireworks, and later had to be licensed to do this. In addition, to protect children, it has been, for many years, illegal to sell fireworks to a child under fourteen.

Bonfire Boys

As I have often mentioned 5 November was a holiday that many would like to forget in former times. The rough element of the town turned out to do what damage it could to houses and shops and other properties, and the law did little or nothing to stop this. Tar barrels were lighted and rolled about the streets, fireworks let off without regard to human safety, and bonfires were often lit between houses causing widespread fires. In Lewes in 1847 the *Sussex Advertiser* whose editor was opposed to the harm done on Bonfire night, published this parody of the Bonfire song in his paper on 2 November, as a warning to the revellers. Here are the last lines:

> *Remember, my boys, remember,*
> *No rum is allowed at 'the Jug',*
> *And the private rooms in December*
> *Are decidedly cool though snug!*
> *Whoever finds winter quarters there*
> *Will remember the 5th for the future I'll swear.*
> *On the 'tottle of the whole' then,*
> *'Twere best to avoid the din,*
> *Let everyone of the bold men*
> *Keep fast his doors within;*
> *Lest he finds too late when regrets are no use,*
> *For the sake of Fawkes, he's been made a great goose.*

This meant that prison was not so comfortable especially in December and that it would be better for the rebels to curtail activities and stay within the law on Bonfire night.

Gradually the gangs known as Bonfire Boys, joined themselves into clubs and became a little more organised and respectable. In Lewes in 1853 processions were started, bands were asked to play, and the Bonfire Boys themselves decided to wear a uniform, consisting of a Guernsey shirt of blue and white horizontal stripes. However for many years the unruly behaviour of the gangs continued, and the editor of the *Sussex Advertiser*, whose name was Peter Bacon, made many attacks through his paper on the proceedings. One Bonfire night his effigy was burnt in the shape of a pig.

As stated previously the hatred in Lewes for the Catholic

religion was very strong, and the story of an incident which happened in 1857 illustrates this. The daughter of one of the Protestant ministers, one Reverend Scobell, was a nun and lived in a convent some miles away from the town. When still a young woman she died of scarlet fever and her body was brought to the town, to be interned in the family vault in All Saints church, by a man called Reverend Neal and a party of nuns — all Catholics of course. After the funeral Reverend Neal asked for entrance to the vault but was prevented by a large crowd who had gathered for the funeral. They shouted, 'No Popery', kicked and scuffed the Catholic churchman and also threatened the nuns who had come to witness the internment. The sisters of mercy escaped to the comparative safety of the railway station while the Reverend Neal took refuge in the King's Head. He was attacked there by several hundred people but managed to escape over a high wall at the back. He and the nuns returned to their own town without witnessing the internment.

Various bonfire societies sprang up in Lewes as they did in other towns, and in time the bonfire celebrations became respectable and the unruly element was lost. This was partly due to the fact that Queen Victoria, deploring the riots, cancelled the public holiday which had been maintained for well over three hundred years, and turned 5 November into an ordinary working day. This of course curtailed activities until the evening and energy was channelled into more constructive pursuits. Carnivals were arranged, bands were asked to play, tableaux depicting scenes from British history became popular. The uniforms of the Bonfire Boys were replaced by fancy dress suitable for the proceedings. Bonfire clubs decided to raise money for various charities which gave the whole proceedings much greater dignity. To do this, Lewes bonfire clubs and those in other towns held whist drives, jumble sales, etc. throughout the year.

During the last two world wars the Plot was not celebrated for security reasons. Before the last war, in Lewes, Hitler was often portrayed as an effigy in the town — a wolf in grandmother's clothing. In 1958 about four thousand torches were made at Lewes out of tow, which were wound onto the ends of sticks about two feet long with wire. On the night they were soaked in paraffin which gave a good light for about twenty minutes. Many townspeople then joined in the torchlight procession which preceded the celebrations.

From early days it was well known that people living in the west country bore special loyalty to the crown, and so it was with a fervour unsurpassed that they celebrated the overthrow of the Gunpowder Plot. Bridgwater has always been one of the ardent contributors. As in other towns, gangs and riots were gradually replaced by more organised and civilised proceedings. The making of Bridgwater squibs was world famous and competitions to ascertain the best home-made firework of the year were very well supported, but as stated the dangers were great and the inhabitants reluctantly agreed to hand over their secret formulas to a manufacturer, who did his best to make the squibs come up to former standards.

Guy Fawkes day in Bridgwater in 1883 was a red letter day and remembered for many years. For as well as the usual carnival, processions and concerts, an extra attraction was the opening of a new bridge over the river Parret, a piece of engineering of which the Bridgwater people were particularly proud. That year the carnival surpassed all others. The torch light procession in which all the community took part was accompanied by four bands! The leading features of the show were a fully rigged ship intended to represent HMS *Arethusa* and a marvellous effigy of Guy Fawkes. Both of these were on trolleys drawn by horses. The guy was more than six feet high and was mounted on a pedestal. He was dressed in a scarlet tunic, short blue breeches, white stockings, a hat with feathers and a black beard and moustache. He wore a sword and carried a torch, and had a lantern slung around his waist. He was followed by 15 men masquerading as knights of the Garter all correctly dressed in the costume of James I's era.

Carnival concerts have always been a great attraction at Bridgwater. All costumes and scenery are home-made and of a very high standard. The different Bonfire clubs with such fascinating names as North Pole, Devonshire Arms, Malt Shovel, West End, Crown and so on have done much to uphold the great carnival tradition. Before the war the Great Western railway ran a day return excursion to Bridgwater from London to give people the opportunity to see for themselves the carnivals at Bridgwater on 5 November; the return fare was 7s 6d (41p).

Hundreds of people each year travelled west to see the world famous event. Another old custom was for masqueraders dressed in all sorts of fancy dress to come onto the platform at Bridgwater station and meet the night mail train from London. They gave the astonished passengers a grand display of Bridgwater squibs. Just before the outbreak of the last war the BBC transmitted a worldwide broadcast from Bridgwater about bonfire celebrations.

GUY FAWKES DAY CUSTOMS
Recipes

Adhering to the tradition of cooking potatoes in the embers of the fire on Bonfire night children might like to make up a guy out of potatoes to cook in this way.

Ingredients:

2 potatoes one larger than the
  other
a wedge of cheese
tinfoil

4 lolly sticks (wooden)
cocktail sticks (wooden)
a few currants and pieces of
  carrot for the face

Method. Scrub the potatoes well, cut a slit in each, insert a slice of cheese and join together with a cocktail stick — one end into the 'body' and the other into the 'head'. Make a slit with a knife to insert lolly sticks for limbs, fix currants for eyes and pieces of carrot for nose and make a mouth with small pieces of cocktail sticks. Wrap up well in tinfoil. Make a cradle out of the rest of the foil and place the 'guy' in the hot ashes of the fire for about an hour depending on the constancy of the heat. Children should use gloves and a stick to take the cooked potatoes out of the ashes, and also of course when unwrapping the foil.

Although a recipe has never been found for 'Tom Trot' the kind of toffee Bella Brown made, an ancient recipe called *Plot Toffee* was found in *The Dalesman's* book, *Yorkshire Cookery,* and this may be similar. Children would enjoy making this — and here is the recipe.

Ingredients:

1 lb (500 g) demerara sugar
4 ozs (100 g) butter or
  margarine
4 ozs (100 g) treacle

1 tablespoonful vinegar
1 tablespoonful water
1 tablespoonful milk

Potato guys.

Method. Bring all the ingredients except the vinegar to the boil, stirring all the time. Keep simmering for fifteen to twenty minutes, still stirring to prevent sticking or burning, until the mixture becomes brittle when a little is dropped into a cup of cold water. Stir in the vinegar and pour into well greased shallow tins. When nearly set score deeply with a knife into conveniently sized squares. Eat while around the bonfire.

Parkin and Thor cakes are made in the North of England on 'Plot' day and here are the recipes, firstly the *Parkin*, from *The Dalesman's* book, *Yorkshire Cookery*.

Ingredients:

½ lb (220 g) flour	10 ozs (260 g) treacle
½ lb (220 g) medium oatmeal	3 ozs (75 g) lard
¼ lb (100 g) soft brown sugar	1 teaspoon bicarbonate of soda
½ teaspoon ginger	about ¼ pint (125 ml) milk

Method. Mix together the flour, oatmeal and ginger. Melt the sugar, lard and treacle and add a little of the milk, in a pan. Pour this into the dry ingredients and mix to a stiff batter. Add the bicarbonate of soda dissolved in the rest of milk. Mix quickly and pour into a well greased shallow tin approx. 11x9x2 inches (28x23x5 cms). The tin may be lined with greaseproof paper if desired. Bake for about an hour, or until firm, at Regulo mark 2 or 300°F.

Thor cakes are similar to Parkin but are baked as a biscuit rather than a cake.

Ingredients:

1 lb (500 g) oatmeal	1 lb (500 g) sugar
¾ lb (375 g) butter	1 lb (500 g) treacle
2 ozs (50 g) candied peel	1 teaspoon coriander or
2 teaspoons baking powder	carraway seeds
1 teaspoon salt	1 teaspoon ground ginger
1 lb (500 g) flour	

Method. Rub butter into dry ingredients and add warm treacle. Knead a little and roll out fairly thinly on a floured board. Cut into rather large rounds with cutter and bake in a moderate oven for about ten minutes. Half quantities may be made.

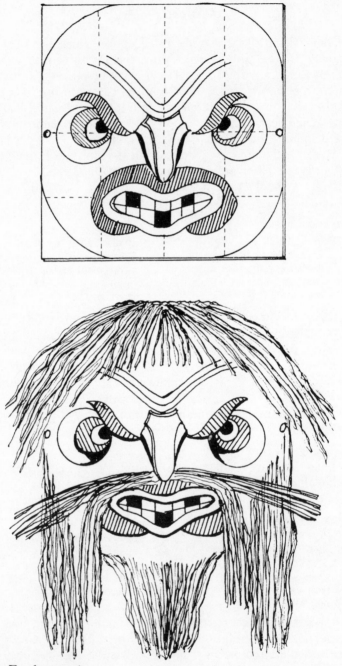

Guy Fawkes mask.

Things For Children To Do

Masks. It has been said that Guy Fawkes blackened his face so as not to be seen easily as he crouched beside the gunpowder barrels. People took to blacking the faces of their guys in the same manner or putting masks on them before burning. Children then adopted the idea of wearing masks themselves as they collected money for their guy. Here are the instructions for making a mask.

Materials needed:

a piece of fairly stiff cardboard about 12 inches (30 cms) square
strips of black or brown paper or strands of wool for hair

pieces of coloured cotton wool for beard and moustache
crayons or felt tip pens
a yard (a metre) of elastic
scissors and glue

Children should draw a large face on the cardboard and cut it out. They should measure it against their faces to see that it fits and make marks to show where eyes, nose and mouth should be drawn. Then draw in these features and cut them out, outlining them with crayons. Drawn eyelashes and eyebrows make the face look more realistic, and strips of wool or paper stuck across the forehead and down the sides of the mask create the hair effect. Cotton wool stuck on for a beard and moustache complete the mask. Two holes made at the side and elastic looped through and tied at the back to fit the head make the mask secure.

Children might make *Guy dolls* like those made years ago and here is what they would need:

a piece of material plain or flesh coloured about 6 inches (15 cms) square and four other pieces measuring 2x3 inches (5x7½ cms)

needle and cotton and a piece of string
crayons or paints
wool for hair
doll's clothes
shoe box with doll's blanket

Method. Fold the largest piece of material into two and sew along the long side and one of the short sides. Turn inside out and stuff with nylon pieces until quite firm. Sew up the remaining side. Do likewise with the smaller pieces and stuff and sew up the remaining seams. A body, arms and legs have now been made. To

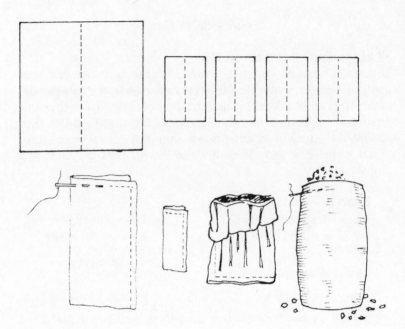

Small doll Guy.

make the head, tie a piece of string a third of the way down the largest bag and pull tightly to make the neck. Sew on arms and legs and paint or draw a face, then glue or sew hair out of pieces of wool into position. Next dress the doll either in doll's clothes, or if children preferred they could make their own clothes to fit the rag doll. A doll dressed in the traditional clothes of Guy Fawkes would look effective. Prepare the shoe box and arrange the doll in it, on the blanket. A competition might be held to select the best doll.

The Dark Lantern.
Materials needed:

a piece of black stiff cardboard
  approximately 12x12 inches
  (30x30 cms)
another piece measuring
  approximately 11x8 inches
  (28x20 cms)
a circle of black paper 6 inches
  (15 cms) in diameter

a strip of black paper 1x6
  inches (2½x15cms)
2 pieces of red shiny paper
  approximately 4x2 inches
  (10x5 cms)
glue and cotton

Method. Using the largest piece of cardboard which will make the outside of the lantern, cut out two oblongs on each side approximately 4x2 inches (10x5 cms) – these will be the spaces which will show 'the glass' or red paper. Glue the long sides so that they overlap to form a tube. Make the bottom by standing the tube in the centre of the circular piece of paper and draw round the outside of the tube. The drawn circle should be about an inch (2½ cms) from the edge of the paper. Cut up to the drawn circle all the way round at one inch (2½ cms) intervals, so that a kind of frill is formed. Dab the circle and cut pieces with glue, then standing the tube in the centre, stick the cut pieces to it to make the bottom of the lantern. To make the inside of the lantern take the other piece of black cardboard (slightly smaller) and glue it to form a tube shape. Then slide it into the first tube and mark where the window cuts have been made. Take out the tube and stick red pieces of paper to correspond with the window shapes. Put the inner tube in again and turn it until the red paper shows in the right places — to look as if the lantern was 'alight'. Thread cotton across the diameter of the inner tube at the top, so that it can be twisted quickly by pulling the cotton, thus removing the red paper from the window cuts and making it a 'dark' lantern by only showing black paper. Glue the handle strips onto each side of the top of the lantern.

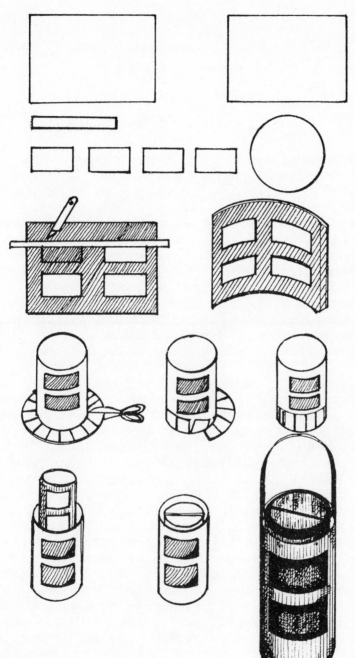

Dark lantern.

CHRISTMAS — 25 DECEMBER

It is common knowledge in the Christian world that the festival of Christmas remembers the birth of Christ on 25 December and that he was the Son of God, who had a human mother, Mary. The birth of Christ is also known as the Incarnation which comes from the Latin word meaning 'flesh'. Christians believe that Christ lived the life of a human being on this earth for the salvation of the world. This together with the Resurrection at Eastertide forms the basis of the Christian religion.

Christmas has now become the most important of the Christian festivals, having superceded Easter during the past century. This is probably due to the fact that the celebrations included the giving of presents. This custom has been commercialised to such an extent that the true meaning of Christmas is often forgotten, particularly in a world where religion does not command the power it did in the past.

The everyday rituals which we associate with Christmas are of pagan origin and are much older than the birth of Christ. One of these rituals was practised in Rome every 25 December or thereabouts by pagan emperors. We know that in AD 274 the Emperor Aurelian celebrated the birthday of the unconquered sun — which after the shortest day and the longest night begins again to give more light to the world. This festival was called Saturnalia or Natalis Invicti — the birthday of the Unconquerable One, and was part of the Winter solstice. All over the world people watched the sun's behaviour with anxiety — their very existence depended on the sun's power and warmth. Therefore it was with much rejoicing that they welcomed the gradual return to lighter and warmer days. Many agricultural customs are linked with this celebration and it was a time of merrymaking and exchanging of presents. Houses were decorated with evergreens just as they are today, and the poor and needy together with the children received presents at this festive season which was continued into the New Year.

At the same time another pagan custom was being celebrated in Germany, Norway, Sweden, Denmark and Greenland. As the Teutonic tribes penetrated Gaul (France) and Britain, the Yule rites began to appear in old Celtic customs — especially in the Druid culture. The lighting of the Yule log was the most important part of the winter festival in pagan times because it honoured the god Thor, and symbolised warmth and light and the continuance of life. Yule candles were lit for the same reason. This feast held to celebrate Thor's festival was called 'Juul' and this is where the word Yule comes from. Evergreens were used to decorate houses and were thought to bring good luck and symbolise everlasting life. Special food and drink were prepared including Yule cake and cider mead. In the old Cornish and Bretagne languages the word for sun was Hiaul or Houl, and this too seems to be connected with the word Yule.

The gospels of St Matthew and St Luke in the New Testament tell of the birth of Jesus Christ. St Luke records — 'In those days there went out a decree from Caesar Augustus that all the world should be taxed'. We know that Mary and Joseph journeyed to pay their taxes and how Jesus was born in a stable at Bethlehem. The birth of Christ was announced by the angels to the shepherds and they, like everyone else went to pay their respects and take gifts to the newly born King.

The idea of the sun bringing returning light and warmth to the world coincided with the Christian concept of Christ being 'The Light of the World' as portrayed in traditional paintings of Christ with a halo. This promised light, hope and everlasting life, to those who believed in him.

The song of the angels was called Nowell and this is remembered in the word Noel — which is French for Christmas. The British name for this festival is simply Christ Mass meaning Holy Communion which is held in honour of Christ's birthday. In many churches this Mass is held traditionally at midnight on 24 December so that the worshippers can enter Christmas Day happily.

Even though we assume that Christ was born in the year AD 1 it is not certain that this is strictly true, as there are no written texts to prove it, so we do not know for sure whether 25 December was in fact the birthday of Christ. Early Christians in the western hemisphere believed that Christ was born round about this time and the western church decided to make 25 December his official birthday as it coincided with the pagan feasts of the Winter solstice, and pagan people would find it easier to go on celebrating on the same day as they had done for hundreds of years. The eastern church however went on celebrating 6 January as Christ's birthday, and it was not until the fifth century that all the Christian sects except one decided to make 25 December the official date and extend the festivities until 6 January. This would honour the baptism of Christ and also the visit of the Magi, the three kings of the east who were supposed to have seen the baby Jesus 12 days after his birth — this celebration is called Epiphany. The sect which still recognises 6 January as Christ's birthday is the Armenian church. The fact that the period of Christmas is called the Twelve Days of Christmas is thereby explained, and we have an old carol to bear witness to this.

Advent
Advent is accepted as the period of waiting before Christmas — before the birth of Christ, and begins on 1 December. Also it marked the beginning of the Christian year in former times.

Before the Reformation when Henry VIII introduced the Protestant church to this country, nearly everyone was Catholic and people used to visit houses prior to Christmas carrying Advent images — models of the Virgin Mary and the Holy Child. The Advent bearers were usually women and it was considered very unlucky if one did not see the Advent images before Christmas. Also everyone was bound to give the holders of the Advent images a halfpenny. The bearers would sing a special carol called the Carol of the Seven Joys at each house they visited. Here is the first of the verses:

> *The first good joy that Mary had,*
> *It was the joy of one;*
> *To see the Blessed Jesus Christ*
> *When he was first her Son;*
> *When he was first her Son, good man,*
> *And blessed may He be,*
> *Both Father, Son and Holy Ghost,*
> *To all eternity.*

An old proverb, now long forgotten said, 'As unhappy as a man who has not seen the Advent images'. Nowadays no-one brings round the Advent images, but Advent calendars are very popular with children in some parts of the country. These calendars probably originated from the old Advent custom and consist of a charming Christmas scene with 24 numbered doors in the picture. One door is opened each day starting on 1 December and ending with Christmas Eve. Each door reveals a different Christmas 'image' until the door marked 24 is opened and in traditional calendars shows the same picture each time — Mary and Joseph looking at the baby Jesus asleep in the manger.

It seems that Advent calendars were first produced in Germany around 1890 and arose from a very pleasant custom of present giving to children prior to Christmas — to teach them the Advent days. On a large wall calendar for December there were 24 squares each having a small door which revealed a small gift when opened. Today Advent calendars can be bought in Britain as in Germany —there are basically two kinds. One sort contains 24 small pictures or images, and a more expensive variety has chocolate in each square as well as a picture. Some German families still like to make their own advent calendars with small gifts as people did years ago. In Germany also, the four Sundays during Advent are marked by the lighting of the Advent wreaths — crowns of evergreens decorated with small objects and candles.

In Sweden the great Advent festival is St Lucia's day — 13 December — and is sometimes called Little Yule. It is closely connected with the Winter festivals and the lighting of fires and candles to celebrate the return of the light and warmth of the sun. In every Swedish village there was a Lucia Queen or Bride. This was a young girl chosen to wear white and who had also a crown of lighted candles upon her head. Her job was to rise very early and take trays of food and coffee to houses and farmsteads in her area. She had in addition to visit all the animal sheds and stables and she symbolised the coming of light and prosperity to all humans and animals alike. She was accompanied by a man on horseback and a long procession of young people carrying lighted candles and dressed as maids of honour, Biblical characters and trolls and demons representing the triumph of good over evil — the return of the sun's power and the defeat of darkness.

Sometimes families had their own Lucia Queen, usually the youngest daughter, who rose early on 13 December put on her white gown and crown of lighted candles and brought food and coffee to each member of the family. These customs are still practised today to a certain extent. St Lucia was a Christian who was martyred for her faith in the fourth century and probably had little to do with the Winter festivals.

St Thomas' day — 21 December was another saint day remembered during Advent. Children took part in the same 'barring out' customs in schools on this day as they did on Shrove Tuesday. They arrived at school early and barricaded themselves in, not letting the master enter. He then declared a holiday as a matter of course.

Another custom on St Thomas' day was to go 'Thomassing' — this meant women of poor families going from door to door begging for wheat and flour with which to make bread and cakes at Christmas time. Most people gave generously and in return received a sprig of holly or mistletoe as a good luck emblem.

St Nicholas and Santa Claus
6 December is the feast day of St Nicholas and it is known that he was bishop of Myra, a town on the south coast of Turkey during the fourth century. Some say he was martyred for his faith during the reign of the Roman emperor, Diocietian, but others maintain that he was one of the few saints who were not martyred and achieved world wide popularity after his natural death.

During his lifetime St Nicholas proved himself to be very fond of children and young people in general, and it is not hard to see how he became patron saint of children or how his fame spread quickly over the rest of the civilised world. There are three famous stories connected with this saint. The earliest tells of three officers unjustly condemned to death, but saved when St Nicholas appeared in a dream to the Emperor Constantine I, and told him of their plight. The emperor then proceeded to free the innocent victims.

The second tells of how in the town where St Nicholas lived there dwelt three sisters with their father, who was so poor that he had no money for dowries, the marriage settlements which were made in those days. The only alternative was to let the three young girls become prostitutes and earn their living that way. When the saint heard of this he was determined to further their marriages. So one dark night he crept to the hut where they were living and threw in a bag of gold intended for a dowry for the eldest daughter. She accepted the gift gratefully. A few nights later he threw in another bag of gold across the threshold and the second daughter knew it was for her dowry. The father could not think who it was who was being so generous to his daughters, and made up his mind to sit up every night to watch who would bring a bag of gold for his third daughter. One night his patience was rewarded for he saw plainly that it was St Nicholas who brought the last bag of gold. The father was so grateful for the dowries that he told everyone what had happened and soon the whole town knew of the good deed. His daughters were soon respectably married and lived happily ever after.

The last story can only be described as a fairy story but is fascinating all the same. It seems that a nobleman sent his three young sons to Athens to be educated. They were to pass through Myra and pay a call on the bishop, St Nicholas, whose kindness to children was well known. The boys reached the town late one evening and they decided to stay the night at an inn, intending to see St Nicholas in the morning. During the night the innkeeper, seeing the boys came from a well-to-do family, killed them for their clothes and the money they were carrying, chopped up the bodies and put the pieces in a pickling barrel in which he was pickling some pork pieces. The innkeeper thought that his crime would never be discovered but St Nicholas saw what happened in a dream that very night, and he awoke, dressed and went straight to the inn. He aroused the innkeeper and accused him of the crime. The innkeeper fell on his knees and begged for mercy and showed where he had hidden the bodies. At once the saint prayed to God to give him strength to restore the dead children to life. His prayers were answered and they arose out of the barrel fit and well. They were blessed by the bishop and sent on their way to Athens and everyone marvelled at the miracle that had been brought about. The custom of electing a boy bishop to take charge of services in cathedrals from St Nicholas' day to Holy Innocents day, 28 December, is thought to have its origin in the above story.

Child choristers selected a suitable junior from their ranks to carry out all the duties of a bishop except Mass. Often their dress was more splendid and more ornate than the bishop's own robes. People took satisfaction from this custom and in London the adult bishop arranged for the child bishop and his youthful attendants to ride through the streets on horseback, which made the ritual even more popular with the common people. They said with satisfaction, 'St Nicholas yet goeth about the City'. In Salisbury cathedral there is a famous monument representing a boy bishop in episcopal dress. The custom of the boy bishop was also held in remembrance of Holy Innocents day — 28 December when Herod had all the male babies slain after the birth of the baby Jesus. The custom of the boy bishop gradually died out as saint days became less important in this country, but at the beginning of this century the ritual was revived in a modified form in Eastbourne and other places. Since that time however the custom seems to have ceased altogether.

St Nicholas died on 6 December 326 and his shrine can be seen in Myra today. He was patron saint of sailors too, and in 1087 Italian sailors took his remains from Myra to Baris in Apulia and this became one of the most popular pilgrimage centres. Devotion to St Nicholas spread all over Europe and he became patron saint of Russia and Lorraine as well as many merchant guilds.

Churches were dedicated to him, there were over 400 in Britain alone, and many Christian names and surnames have their derivations in the word Nicholas. The church of St Nicholas situated in Lombard Street in London, which had on its spire three gold balls commemorating the three bags of gold that St Nicholas gave away in the legend, was burnt down in the Great Fire of London in 1666 and never rebuilt. However the sign of the three gold balls has been used as a trade mark for money lenders and pawn brokers since that time, and they had their headquarters in Lombard Street for many years.

Netherland Protestants, settling in New Amsterdam (New York) brought a new name for the feast day of St Nicholas — for in Dutch he is known as Sinter Class or San Klaas. English speaking people soon called the kind benevolent magician who gave presents to children at Christmas time Santa Claus, and his fame spread quickly all over America.

After the Reformation when many countries became Protestant many of the Catholic saint days were either forgotten or moved. So the feast of St Nicholas on 6 December was amalgamated with Christmas day, and this is another reason why presents are given to children on Christ's birthday. In some Catholic countries however, children still hang up their stockings on St Nicholas' eve and receive presents and sweets. In America children write their request letters to St Nicholas on 6 December, hoping for the right kind of presents for Christmas.

In Switzerland and Germany, St Nicholas is depicted as a bishop wearing bishop's clothing at Christmas time. In southern Germany the bishop is accompanied by 12 fierce looking people dressed in straw cloaks and wearing masks or animal heads and carrying clanging cowbells. These friends enter each house with Santa Claus and pretend to punish naughty children amid much laughter and merriment, and after the presents have been given out they pretend to drive everyone from the room and have the presents for themselves.

In some Swiss villages there is a procession before the arrival of Santa Claus. People dressed in strange attire — as demons, flourishing whips, a watchman blowing a bugle, a man dressed in black wearing horns and another as a goat, who bleats outside all the houses to tell people that the procession is passing. Next comes Santa's servant carrying a sack in which he threatens to put all naughty children and lastly comes Santa and banishes all the demons and bad men of the company and distributes sweets and toys to the children.

In the Netherlands children leave their wooden clogs filled with hay for St Nicholas' horse when he comes riding by. In France children leave their wooden clogs on the hearth on Christmas Eve, for they believe that it is the Christ child himself that brings the presents.

All these traditions of present giving to children have a long history in Europe and in America, but in Britain children had no magical figure to bring them presents at Christmas but knew that the presents were given to them by their families. That is until about a hundred years ago when Father Christmas first appeared, but this is a different story and will be dealt with later.

Christmas Carol
The customary time for singing carols was from St Thomas' day,

21 December, until about 9 a.m. on Christmas Day. In the past each county had its own traditional carols called 'curls'. As most people were illiterate these 'curls' were learnt by heart and handed down from generation to generation. The carol singers were organised into separate choirs, and the plan of the evening was carefully worked out so that the bigger houses expected the singers at an appropriate time and were ready to welcome them with refreshment and hot drinks. Often the singers were composed of church choirs and gave good renderings of favourite carols before being entertained and rewarded in the warmth of a large kitchen.

At first the word 'carol' meant a ring dance because early carollers danced in a ring while singing their joyful songs. For each carol, although primarily a religious song, was usually sung at most feast and festival days throughout the year. Carols were sung at Mayday, Eastertide and Whitsuntide as well as at Christmas in former times.

Carols can usually be divided into four kinds. The lively, happy song such as 'Ding Dong Merrily on High', the lullabies such as 'Away in a Manger' — sometimes called Luther's Cradle Song, the more solemn hymn-like carol such as 'It came upon a Midnight Clear' — and the non-religious such as 'Good King Wenceslas'. This song tells that on the Feast of Stephen, 26 December, Wenceslas performed a miracle that has never been forgotten. Most people will be surprised to learn that contrary to belief this carol is only just over a hundred years old. The words were written by Reverend J.M. Neale and set to a tune found in an ancient Spring carol songbook dated 1582 which originated in Sweden.

Another popular secular carol is 'The Twelve Days of Christmas'. This is thought to be very old and may have French connections.

Most of the older carols had their origins in mummers' plays and the famous Coventry Carol is one of these. It begins 'Lulla, lulla thou little tiny child'. This carol is always sung at Christmas in Coventry. Even during the war after the disastrous air raid of 1940 the clergy and choir gathered at Christmas to sing it as usual in the burnt out ruins of the cathedral.

Another old carol found in a book printed in 1521 is the 'Boar's Head Carol'. It was written partly in English and partly in Latin and was sung every year at Queen's College Oxford, when the traditional boar's head associated with Christmas feasting was brought to the table for Christmas dinner. It was decorated with sprigs of rosemary and bay, had an orange in its mouth and was carried in a silver basin by four men while the choir sang:

> *The boar's head in hand bear I,*
> *Bedecked with bays and rosemary,*
> *And I pray you, my master, be merry*
> *Quod estis in convivio. (for you are at a merry banquet.)*

The carol had three verses and a Latin chorus, and when the boar's head finally reached the head of the table the chief singer received the orange from its mouth and the chief guests were given sprigs of rosemary and bay.

At Magdalene College, Oxford, carols used to be sung by the choir on Christmas Eve for the benefit of the townspeople who were allowed into the Great Hall to listen, admire the magnificent Christmas tree and decorations and partake of a special supper, of which the first course was frumenty.

Today the service is held a week before Christmas to allow the choir more holiday time and there is also a service given for the public in the chapel. The hall still has its huge Christmas tree which comes from the college woods at Tubney. After the singing the Founder's Cup filled with hot punch is presented to the president, who wishes everyone a happy Christmas before taking a drink and then passing it round. A buffet supper is served but frumenty is not on the menu.

In Berkshire and Hampshire amongst other counties, it was the custom formerly for the church choir to sing carols from the top of the church tower. This must have presented an impressive entertainment for the local people. In some parts of Yorkshire the choir boys would bring in baskets of rosy apples and present an apple together with a sprig on rosemary to each member of the congregation on Christmas Day.

Even today, some fascinating rituals are performed at Christmas carol gatherings. For instance in Norwich Cathedral and in smaller Parish churches in Norfolk the Christingle service gains popularity year by year. A Christingle is an orange into which a candle has been inserted. The orange is decorated with small nuts and fruits such as raisins or dates and put in place with cocktail sticks, and a red ribbon is tied round the finished product. The candle when lighted symbolises the light of the world, which is Christ himself, the nuts and fruit represent the fruits of the earth, the orange represents the world and the red ribbon the blood of Christ. Up to 600 children each with a lighted Christingle attend the cathedral carol service, and walk slowly up and down the aisles between the packed pews, while carols are being sung. Then at a given moment the bishop says, 'And there came a mighty wind and blew the candles out'. At this moment all the children blow out their candles and it indeed makes a mighty wind, much to the delight and entertainment of the onlookers.

Wassailing
Wassailing and its customs date back to early times. The Saxon words 'Wass Hael' which mean 'to your health' were called out by the Saxon overlord of the household when he bade everyone drink the hot mead or ale in the large wooden bowl kept especially for this purpose. This was the custom at the beginning of each year, and after the master himself had drunk the toast, the bowl would be passed on to the next important person in the household, and so on until the least important had had their share.

When families no longer lived under the lord's roof but in their own often humble homes, the custom of the peasants going a-wassailing at Christmas and New Year was carried on. They took the empty wassailing bowl as they were usually unable to fill it themselves, decorated it with evergreens and tinsel, and went from house to house of their wealthier neighbours begging for food and drink to fill the bowl. This bowl was known as the wassail cup and those carrying it would sing a song outside the house, something like a Christmas carol. Here are five verses from a wassailing song sung by children:

> *Here we come a-wassailing*
> *Among the leaves so green,*
> *Here we come a-wassailing*
> *So fair to be seen.*

Our wassailing cup is made
Of the rosemary tree
And so is your best beer
Out of the best barley.

We are not daily beggars,
That beg from door to door,
But we are neighbours' children
Whom you have seen before.

God bless the master of this house,
Likewise the mistress too,
And all the little children
That round the table go.

Good master and good mistress,
While sitting round your fire,
Pray think of us poor children
Who are wandering in the mire.

This is a song that adult wassailers used to sing outside each of the larger houses in the district:

Wassail! Wassail! All over town,
Our bread is white, our ale is brown;
Our bowl is made of the mapling tree
We be all good fellows who drink to thee.

Here's to old Dobbin and to his right eye;
God send our mistress as good Christmas pie;
As good Christmas pie as e'er we did see —
With our wassailing bowl we would drink to thee.

Here's to Filpail and her long tail
God send our master us never may fail
Of a cup of good beer, we pray you draw near
And then you shall hear our jolly wassail.

Be there any maids, we suppose there is some,
They'll not let young men stand on the cold stone.
Sing hey, oh ye maids, come troll back the pin,
And the fairest of all shall let us come in.

Come butler, come bring us a bowl of the best,
And we hope then in heaven your soul it shall rest,
But if you shall bring us a bowl of the small —
Then down fall the butler, the beer, bowl and all!

Sometimes the wassail bowl was filled with a drink called 'Lamb's Wool', a mixture of hot beer, wine, honey and spices with cream and a hot apple dropped into the mixture.

A wassailing custom which has connections with the Advent images became known as the Vessel Cup ritual. Children and adults would go from house to house carrying one or two dolls in a box, representing the Virgin Mary and the Christ Child. The dolls were usually beautifully dressed and the box tastefully decorated with evergreens, paper flowers, ribbons and clean linen. The custom was also known as the 'doll in the box'. The bearers would sing a special carol known as the 'Holy Well' beginning with the lines:

It was under the leaves and the leaves of life;
It was a bright holiday.
Sweet Jesus, he asked his Mother's leave
If he might go to play.

In some parts of the country this carol is known as the 'Withy Twig' and is accepted as being very old. Sometimes the bearers sang 'The Seven Joys of Mary' as did the bearers of the Advent images centuries before, and in the same way. It was considered very bad luck not to contribute something to the wassailers.

Another form of wassailing performed around Christmas was the blessing of the apple orchards to ensure a good crop the following year. Wassailers would gather round a large apple tree at dusk, sing songs and pour cider over the roots of the tree, and then make as much noise as they could with saucepans, horns, guns and shouting to frighten off any evil spirits which may have been lurking round, waiting to do damage to the ensuing crop. Then the wassailers, their mission accomplished, would return to the warmth of the farmhouse kitchen and spend the rest of the evening eating, drinking and merrymaking.

Christmas Eve

The most important function on Christmas Eve in former times was the bringing in and lighting of the Yule log. This custom originated in pagan times when every dwelling large or small had its traditional Yule log. Small cottages with only one room burnt as large a log as they could fit into the grate, and in the bigger houses the fireplaces were often over six feet wide, built especially to accommodate the Yule log at Christmas time. The log or clog as it was sometimes called was part of a tree trunk often decorated with ribbons and evergreens, and dragged into place by chains. It was kindled with a piece of log saved from the previous year for luck. While dragging the heavy log and pushing it into place the boys from the village would chant, 'Yule, Yule, a pack of new cards and a Christmas stool.'

The heat from the Yule log was tremendous and at first it was impossible to sit within two yards of it. It was usual for it to burn throughout the week of festivities without going out.

In some parts of the country such as Devonshire the ashen faggot or brand was burnt. This consisted of many branches of the green ash bound together by strong binders. Ash wood was very popular as not only did the green wood burn well, but it was supposed to protect the household from evil. Everyone sat and watched the faggot burn and when a binder snapped it was a signal for the master of the house to open another gallon of home brewed cider.

The lighting of the Yule candle was another important part of the ritual of Christmas Eve. Cottagers saved moulten grease or fat and poured it into a mould to solidify, which was then removed before use; the Yule candle referred to was often a large mould candle and was usually about 18 inches long. The candle was placed in the centre of the table and it was considered very unlucky if it went out during the Christmas holidays. The candles were often coloured red, sometimes blue or green, and were decorated with evergreens such as ivy and holly. In Derbyshire miners used to sit round the Yule candle on this night and drink posset — a kind of ale mixed with milk and nutmeg. They passed round the bowl and supped the drink with a large communal spoon.

Frumenty, which I mentioned in the Eastertide section, was frequently made and drunk on Christmas Eve. This consisted of a dish of wheat grains soaked in water overnight and then boiled in sweetened milk and flavoured with spices until thick and creamy. Hot elderberry wine was a traditional Christmas drink as well as large quantities of ale and cider. In the Shetland islands they drank Whipcoll — consisting of egg yolks beaten with sugar to which cream had been slowly added, then the whole flavoured with rum or brandy.

Another traditional dish served on Christmas Eve was the huge Christmas pie. This is not to be confused with mince pies with which we are so familiar. It was made up of beef, tongue, fowls, eggs, sugar, raisins, lemon and orange peel and different kinds of spices. It was cooked in a large pastry case too large to fit into a tin and the shape was kept firm during the cooking by iron bands. It was called a pestle pie and often weighed over a hundredweight. Families were larger then and visitors were many, so this pie was something of a 'standby' for the holiday and saved the cook of the house much work.

Years ago, small dolls modelled out of left over scraps of pastry were made on Christmas Eve and given as presents to children on Christmas Day. The shapes were decorated with currants to represent eyes, and perhaps hair, with small pieces of candied peel or glacé cherries for the mouth and nose. They were often presented in a box decorated as a doll's crib with clean linen, lace and ribbons. When the pastry doll had been eaten then the crib was used for a real doll's cradle.

The activities on Christmas Eve always included the telling of ghost stories and the playing of cards, and of course the very pleasurable pastime of eating and drinking. At twelve o'clock, midnight, the 'lucky bird' was expected to cross the threshold of each home to bring good luck and prosperity to the inmates for the coming year. This custom was called 'first footing' and is still practised on New Year's Eve in modern times, especially in Scotland. In England the 'lucky bird' was the most important visitor on Christmas Day, a dark man was needed to perform the ritual and he usually carried a lump of coal and a piece of bread to symbolise a plentiful supply of both in the coming year. Sometimes a professional 'lucky bird' was hired who would go quickly in and out of houses for a small fee. Whether professional or amateur, it was considered very bad luck not to reward this important visitor in some way or another. It was regarded as very unlucky if a woman crossed the threshold first at this time.

Christmas Day

It seems, according to some of the menus, that everyone in the well-to-do houses over-ate on Christmas Day. Christmas dinner consisted of a vast number of courses. The meal always began with the traditional boar's head followed by Christmas pudding. These two courses were brought in accompanied by loud cheers and blowing of trumpets. The pudding consisted of a kind of porridge boiled in a pan and made out of meat broth thickened with bread crumbs and flavoured with raisins, currants, prunes and spices. Then the real meal began, consisting of beef joints, roasted swans, venison, capons, peacocks and many other dishes. These were followed by various sweetmeats, all washed down with wine and ale.

Pudding cloths were introduced in the eighteenth century and plum porridge became plum pudding, cooked in a cloth in boiling water. When the serving of the boar's head declined owing to the scarcity of boars in this country, turkey and beef replaced it. The popularity of the new plum pudding increased and it became the second main course served after the turkey, as it is today. It was served with brandy poured over and set alight. The Victorians introduced the idea of adding silver charms and sixpences to the pudding, so that delighted children would eat up the rich sweetmeat in order to find a hidden treasure. A ring meant a sweetheart, but a thimble meant another year as an old maid.

Mince pies have a long history and date back to before Elizabethan times. In those days the pies were made with meat as well as dried fruit and spices, and they were oblong in shape, not round like they are today. Some say that the shape of the pastry crust was made to look like the manger. Old cookery books call the pastry the 'coffin' because it was coffin shaped. For every mince pie eaten, which was baked by another, was the promise of a happy month, and this is still believed today.

Many of the poorer families took their Christmas dinners to be cooked at the local bakers. This was because either their own ovens were not big enough, or because they did not possess ovens. Charles Dickens gives an amusing description of the busy comings and goings from the communal ovens in his *Christmas Carol*.

One Christmas Day custom which is entirely modern and is

now firmly established in the Yuletide festivities is the Queen's speech. It was her grandfather King George V who first spoke on Christmas Day to his people over the radio, in 1932. Later his son George VI, the present Queen's father, carried on the tradition, and now it is our present Queen Elizabeth who speaks to her subjects at home and abroad on television and radio.

Boxing Day
The day after Christmas Day is St Stephen's day — 26 December. He was a little known saint who achieved eternal fame by being the first Christian to be martyred for his faith, and he met his death by stoning.

Boxing Day is so called because it was the custom on that day for tradesmen to collect their Christmas boxes or gifts in return for good and reliable service throughout the year. The tradition stems from Roman times when money to pay for athletic games was collected in boxes. Amongst the ruins of Pompeii, boxes made out of earthenware with slits in the top, full of coins have been found. Later the Romans brought the idea of collecting boxes to Britain, and monks and clergy soon used similar boxes to collect money for the poor at Christmas. On the day after Christmas Day, the priests used to open the boxes and distribute the contents to the poor of the village. Thus this day came to be called Boxing Day.

After the Reformation the old Catholic customs were not carried out by the new churchmen. So at Christmas time there were no longer money gifts for the poor. This caused great hardship, to the extent that the destitute and needy took matters into their own hands and visited their richer neighbours, carrying collecting boxes. Later tradesmen and errand boys adopted the idea and this is why to this day we give Christmas boxes to people who have served us well over the year.

Many outdoor sports are associated with Boxing Day. Squirrels were hunted in great numbers centuries ago, until an epidemic reduced their numbers to almost nil. Bird shooting was also held to be good sport, the wren was hunted and an old story tells us that a wren killed on St Stephen's day would protect whoever owned it from shipwreck. Fox and hound hunts were often held on Boxing Day in rural parts of the community.

An interesting old game coming from Sussex and played

hundreds of years ago consisted of men bowling oranges along the highway, an orange hit by another's was forfeited to the successful bowler.

Sports and Games

Apart from the telling of ghost stories and the playing of cards around the fire, Christmas in general meant large family parties who were only too eager to partake in numerous games. One of the most popular which has lasted through the years is the game of *charades,* when syllables of a chosen word are performed, and then the whole word, in a series of sketches, while the rest of the party guesses the word. The game of charades undoubtedly owes its origins to the mummers' plays, and people still find great fun and entertainment in dressing up and generally 'acting the fool!'

Snap dragon was played frequently years ago. The gathering would group themselves round the large kitchen table or sometimes the brick or stone floor, and the largest dish in the house was heaped with raisins and a whole bottle of brandy was poured over them. The lights were put out and the brandy set alight. Blue and yellow flames rose from the fruit and each member of the party tried to snatch the fruit and eat it without receiving burnt fingers or mouths. One had to be quick at this game as one small slip might mean a nasty burn. Snap apple as described in the Hallowe'en chapter was also popular but is not played nowadays as it too is regarded as dangerous.

Forfeit games were popular, and one such game called *Buff* was in great demand. The 'victim' had to remain solemn without one vestige of a smile, while all the others did their best by words and antics to make him smile or laugh. Not surprisingly few survived this test, and so the victim had to pay a forfeit which usually meant a kiss under the kissing bush for each member of the opposite sex. Other games requiring forfeits were spinning the trencher, hunt the slipper, musical chairs, and postman's knock.

In Derbyshire a game called the *Cushion dance* used to be very popular. All young people took part, dancing to the tune of the fiddler, and to determine the partners a large cushion was used on which the swains knelt before their chosen one. On acceptance a boy could expect a kiss and a dance from the girl of his choice. A charming dancing game found in Cornwall was for children, usually girls singing Christmas songs and carols, to dance around lighted candles which had been pushed into tubs of sand on the floor.

Evergreens

Evergreens have been used since early times to decorate houses and temples during Winter festivals. It is not surprising that a number of superstitions have become associated with them over the centuries. Apart from their use in herbal medicine, and as fuel when wood was scarce, it was believed that they brought good luck to the household during the dark months of Winter.

Holly, ivy, bay, yew and laurel were very popular, although it was thought unlucky to leave them up after Twelfth Night — a belief still held today. However, some greenery was kept until Shrove Tuesday when it was used as fuel to cook pancakes. Of all the evergreens the mistletoe has the most interesting history. It was revered by the Druids who thought it had magical properties, as it grew out of branches of trees and did not itself touch the ground. We know now that mistletoe is a parasite, which takes nourishment from other living trees. But to the Druids it was an enigma, and after their Winter sacrifices when humans and animals had been killed to appease the gods of nature, the Druids would cut down the mistletoe from the oak groves and give a small piece to each one of their company as a good luck emblem. The mistletoe twig was then hung over the threshold of dwellings to protect the occupants from death by arrows. This last custom comes from the Norse legend which tells how Baldur the sun god, and second son of Odin and Frigga, went to his mother and told her that he had a premonition that he was going to die. Frigga, the goddess of Nature, summoned all living plants and animals and told them never to hurt Baldur, but she forgot about the mistletoe. Baldur fought bravely after that and was never harmed. His brother Loki was jealous of him and did his best to destroy him. Loki dressed himself up as an old woman and went to Frigga and told her how brave her son Baldur was. Frigga was pleased and flattered and without thinking told the old woman that there was only one thing that could harm Baldur, and that was the mistletoe. Loki went away and made an arrow out of a branch of mistletoe wood and arranged to have Baldur wounded with it, and from this wound he never recovered.

Although it is seldom found in churches owing to its pagan connections, mistletoe is still hung up in houses at Christmas time until this very day. People have always believed that it is bad luck for the plant to touch the floor, and this also has its origins in Druidism. Pieces of mistletoe have also been regarded as good luck charms, and the practice of kissing underneath it to seal a wish is very old, although no-one seems to know why kissing became associated with the plant. Centuries ago the habit of kissing was much more widespread in Britain than it is today. People would kiss each other when they met and again when they parted. The family would kiss each other in the morning and last thing at night. Foreigners were amazed at this custom; and of course at Christmas time kissing became even more popular.

Not every part of the country could obtain mistletoe at Christmas time, as it only grew in certain areas, and transport was poor, so a substitute had to be found — this was the kissing bush or bough. It usually consisted of a small bush of holly or yew uprooted and hung upside down from the kitchen ceiling. It was decorated with rosy apples, oranges, sweetmeats, tinsel, brightly coloured ribbons and small gifts of all kinds. In Devonshire and other western parts of the country, the bush was sometimes dipped in flour and waster paste and left to dry before being hung up and decorated, and this gave the appearance of snow. Sometimes a bough of yew or holly was used and often a more elaborate decoration was made. This usually consisted of two hoops of wire fastened together at right angles — one inside the other, and decorated with ribbons and evergreens and hung with Christmas fruit and gifts. The hoops were kept from year to year, to be decorated afresh each Yuletide. The kissing bush was very popular, everyone in the family had to kiss underneath it at Christmas time, and visitors did likewise.

With the coming of railways mistletoe could be easily distributed to all parts of the country, with the result that mistletoe was universally used and the kissing bush became somewhat rare. Also, the introduction of the Christmas tree in the mid nineteenth century resulted in a further decline of the kissing bush.

The custom of decorating evergreens can be traced back to Roman times. The poet Virgil who lived from 70-19BC described in one of his poems how people decorated pine trees with small objects during the Winter festivals. In the eighth century it is said that St Boniface, the English missionary to Germany, put up a fir tree, hung with small offerings, to the Christ child at Christmas time, to take the place of the sacred oak that was worshipped by the pagans in honour of their god Odin, known in Britain as Woden. Also in Germany during the sixteenth century, Martin Luther is reported as having hung a fir tree with candles at Christmas time.

Owing perhaps to their past history of tree decorating, the Germans adopted the custom of 'trimming' fir trees with small objects such as sweets, candles and gifts at Yuletide, but it was not until the last century that the idea was introduced into Britain. Prince Albert, the German husband of Queen Victoria, introduced decorated Christmas trees to Windsor castle at Christmas in 1847, much to the delight of his children. The idea soon became popular and by 1860 the Christmas tree was well established as part of the Christmas celebrations. Germans who emigrated to America took the idea with them where it soon became as popular as it was in this country.

The communal Christmas tree is quite a modern idea and originally came from America. In 1909 an illuminated tree was set up on Mount Wilson in Pasadena, California, and in 1912 one appeared in Madison Square, New York, and soon the custom spread throughout the United States.

In Britain, Christmas trees could be seen decorated in churches and other public places; the two in St Paul's Cathedral by the west door and the gifts that go with them come from the Queen, and the trees are from her Sandringham estate. The most famous Christmas tree in Britain is the one that is given annually by the people of Oslo to the citizens of London and stands in Trafalgar Square, under Nelson's column. This custom was begun in 1947 in commemoration of London's part in the Second World War.

When the use of paper became more widespread the garlands of evergreens and ribbons were copied, and paper decorations and streamers were made. At first it was only the rich houses who could afford these luxuries, but as living standards rose, nearly everyone could afford a few pence to buy paper for trimmings. Many decorations were home-made. Lanterns, bells and intricate streamers became the fashion, and even today we have paper chains which give children hours of fun. The paper decorations were carefully folded and preserved from year to year, a practice which many families still carry out today.

Nature Customs
There are many customs associated with animals and plants during Yuletide. The raven is supposed to have been the first bird to hear of the Nativity, as tradition has it that he was flying over Bethlehem at the time and heard the angels singing. The cock was the first to let the glad tidings be known for he cried 'Christus natus est' — and from that time onwards cocks are supposed to crow all through the night of Christmas Eve. The cow in the stable, it is said, kept the infant Jesus warm with her breath, and from that time onwards her breath has been thought to be sweeter than any other animal. People say that as midnight strikes on Christmas Eve cattle in the field and horses in the stable turn to the East and kneel. Bees are said to hum the Hundredth Psalm in their hives; and all animals are supposed to acquire the power of speech for a short time. It was thought very dangerous to listen to the animals' talk and that dire misfortunes would befall anyone who did so.

On Christmas Eve and, all over the holiday, working animals were given a rest and extra rations in remembrance of Christ's birthday. Horses were often given a drink of ale — or sometimes a piece of Christmas pudding to ensure good health. All domestic poultry were allowed extra rations of corn, and the wild animals and birds were not forgotten. Food and corn were distributed on house tops for birds and in some places a sheaf of corn was tied to church doors for them to feed on. These customs may have arisen out of the teachings of St Francis of Assissi, who lived in the thirteenth century and who is the patron saint of animals.

The origin of our popular Christmas rose may have come from France, where the story goes that it sprang from the ground when the Angel Gabriel touched it with his staff, so that a small girl, who accompanied the shepherds to the stable might have something to give the infant Jesus. Another story states how each shepherd brought a gift but one had nothing to give but a daisy which he picked on the way. When he offered it to the Christ child he touched it with his lips, and the petals turned red at the edges and since then most daises have rose tipped petals.

Legend tells that when Joseph of Aramathea, a disciple of Christ, came to Britain he thrust his staff made of thornwood on Wearyall Hill, Glastonbury where it took root and bloomed every Christmas Eve — which was then 5 January. In 1752 our calendar was put back 11 days to make Britain the same as all other European countries; and the thorn still blossomed on the old Christmas Eve. Some people regarded this as proof that this was the true birthday of Christ. During Puritan times in the mid-seventeenth century the Glastonbury thorn was destroyed but luckily by then several cuttings were thriving in different parts of the country. One can be seen in the ruins of Glastonbury Abbey and another in Orcop in Herefordshire. These hawthorns belong to Winter flowering varieties which bloom twice a year and people are seldom disappointed in their hope of seeing thorn buds opening on 5 January.

One Christmas saying was that if the first rays of sun could be seen through the apple trees on Christmas morning then it meant a very good apple harvest. The weather during the 12 days of Christmas was thought to be very important. An old saying went, 'A green Christmas maketh a full churchyard', meaning that a mild December is often followed by bitterly cold months which was bad news for the old and infirm. Another saying went, 'A green Christmas — a white Easter'. The actual day on which Christmas fell was carefully noted. A Monday Christmas foretold a long hard Winter, but a Wednesday Christmas or a Saturday New Year promised fine weather and a good harvest.

Miracle and Mummers' Plays
On most festival days, people used to look forward to good entertainment from plays performed by either wandering players or locals. There were two sorts; the miracle plays and the mummers' plays.

The miracle plays were religious in content and acted out many different stories from the Bible. These were begun in the ninth century by church people who realised that the ordinary uneducated person could not understand the Bible partly because it was written in Latin, and mainly, because the majority of people at that time were illiterate. A further stumbling block was that the church services were conducted in Latin also. Some enterprising clergy thought of the idea of showing the people the Bible stories by actually acting them out. Later different merchant guilds took up the idea and performed a play each on a special feast day. This custom has now ceased, although the annual Lord Mayor's show in London with its many tableaux presented by numerous companies and services is a last link with the miracle plays.

The other type of play, the mummers' play, is thought to be much older — and was probably in existence long before the arrival of Christianity. These entertainments were performed by the local working people, acting out the stories of the seasons, or the myths and legends of the pagan Norse gods that they knew so well. In all the plays the theme of death and resurrection plays a central part. Usually there is a fight between two of the characters, one is killed but brought back to life by the magical powers of the doctor. Some of these traditional plays grew out of ritualistic dances such as the sword dance.

When people were converted to Christianity the characters of the mummers changed and they became respectable beings acting out stories of right triumphing over evil. The most popular Christmas play was St George and the Dragon. The usual characters taking part were St George, the doctor, the Turk, the Fool or Jester, the Dragon and — Old Father Christmas. The last mentioned character was in charge of proceedings, not only was he master of ceremonies, introducing the play itself and then the players individually, but it seems that he was also stage manager producing props where needed and 'filling in' when others forgot their lines. It is thought by some that Old Father Christmas was modelled on Odin, the father of the Norse gods, who was supposed to fly over the world riding his eight-toed horse Sleipnir, during the Winter festivities and making sure that everyone was enjoying himself. As Odin has always been portrayed as having a long beard and fur trimmed cloak, so Father Christmas has worn this costume since time immemorial and the clothes have not altered.

The word 'mumming' means to disguise and the early players always dressed themselves in unusual clothing, wearing masks or animal heads, or wigs and false beards. A mummer was a masker from the Danish word Mumme or Dutch word Momme for mask. And Momar is the Scillian word for fool. There is an account of mummery performed in 1377 by the citizens of London for the entertainment of Prince Richard, son of the Black Prince. An amazing torchlight procession with people playing trumpets and all sorts of musical instruments, not to mention the mummers dressed in fantastic garb, paraded the streets with much noise and merriment.

Father Christmas
During the Middle Ages it became the custom at Christmas time, in large houses and at the court of the reigning monarch, to appoint a Lord of Misrule. This was a person usually the fool or jester nominated to take charge of the festivities. He had mainly to ensure that everyone had a good time, arrange the entertainment and make sure there was plenty of food available. He arranged practical jokes and things often got out of hand at this time of the year and a topsy turvy state of affairs resulted. Later, with changing religions, this custom was forgotten, but was revived in Victorian times. The Victorians laid great emphasis on Christmas, and large houses with many children appointed a Lord of Misrule — only this time they chose Old Father Christmas, straight out of the mummers' play. He became the spirit of Christmas and represented everything that was jolly, kind and good.

It is clear therefore that the British Father Christmas was not at all the same being as St Nicholas or Santa Claus. As previously mentioned, British children did not have a magical being to bring them presents on Christmas Eve as did children in other countries, and the Victorians felt that they would like to put this right. Gradually Father Christmas became incorporated into the tradition of Christmas.

It was the Christmas card that first associated Father Christmas with present-giving to children. A charming set of cards was published in the late 1860's which showed Father Christmas distributing presents to children. Another card showed him treating adults in the same way. He was portrayed in various activities such as playing snowballs with the children in the garden, or skating on the ice with Mrs Christmas, or just spreading happiness and cheer by his smiling jolly face. As the present-giving Father Christmas image grew, people realised that at last here they had an ideal magical character who could come in the night and leave presents for children. A character who was not borrowed from another country but who was entirely British and whose origin could be traced back into the history of Britain.

As the idea grew the method of transport came under consideration. Firstly another Christmas card publisher portrayed Father Christmas distributing presents to children from a basket under a brightly coloured air balloon — which incidentally was the latest craze in transport in the late Victorian era. But this 'modern' idea did not appeal and later Father Christmas was shown arriving in a gift laden sleigh pulled by reindeers, straight from the North Pole. This image echoed back to the legend of the Norse gods and the god Odin as he rode across the sky on his eight-toed horse. The fact that Norway, Iceland and Greenland were all Scandinavian countries and were lands of ice and snow where reindeers and sleighs were used for transport seems to complete the explanation.

Father Christmas became a national figure and soon was the object of political cartoons. In Punch magazine dated 26 December 1874 he is portrayed sitting hunched up in his own Christmas tree whilst on the ground waiting for him to come down are bird cartoons representing Christmas bills, Christmas boxes, Dinners and Waits — all pointing to the fact that although Christmas is a merry time of the year it prompts people to spend money they do not have, and therefore they have to face the consequences afterwards. Another cartoon published round about the same time shows Father Christmas drenched to the skin holding his umbrella, being welcomed into the warmth of a home by a kindly, buxom lady offering him a drink of hot punch. The lady's name is Mrs. Bull and she is saying 'La! Father Christmas, you've only to get into your dry clothes and take plenty of this, and you'll be merry enough, I warrant!'

But as far as children are concerned a cartoon published in Punch in December 1911, is much more interesting. It shows Father Christmas helping to sell toys to children in the toy bazaar in a big department store. True, there was no sack full of presents or special Father Christmas grotto, but surely it was not long before this idea developed.

In the previous century large shops with toy departments had made great efforts to put on spectacular shows to attract both children and their parents at Christmas time. The original Mr Gamage and his son put on marvellous shows at Christmas time. One year it was a real live circus and another, in 1913, the show was — 'A wonderful Fire Brigade Scene using "real water" '.

Three copies of handbills issued to customers from The Bon Marche stores in Brixton, dated in the 1800's, advertised great attractions for children at the Christmas bazaars. An entertainment was organised and a building hired for the occasion to house as many juveniles as possible. It was stated on all three bills that buyers had scoured the continent to bring back novelties that would delight the young ones. And one year the added attraction was that the whole enterprise was to be 'electrified'.

I was also sent an interesting account of Christmas long ago as remembered by employees of Trewin Brothers of Watford (later under the John Lewis Partnership). It was recorded in the house magazine 'Chronicle' — Christmas 1966 and 1967. Dorothy Glasspool remembered as a child visiting the Christmas grotto held in the basement before 1918. She recalled wonderful scenery using the Jack and the Beanstalk theme. There were caves, rocks, lighted crevices depicting scenes from the pantomime, a giant, Jack and his mother and of course at the end Father Christmas with his sack of toys. Her mother paid sixpence for her to visit the wonderland and receive a present from the sack. She remembered feeling scared of Father Christmas as he wore a shiny red mask which made him less than human in her eyes.

Another account by a Mr F. Masters recalls the time when he was asked to play Father Christmas for Trewins in 1919. He was in charge of the dispatch department at that time as he was responsible for the many parcels which were delivered from Trewins, it must have seemed very appropriate that he should play the part. He was driven around Watford in his regalia on a Saturday afternoon a few weeks before Christmas and arrived at the store at an arranged time to open the enchanted grotto and its caves. He remembered that the crowds were so great on these occasions (this became a tradition) that policemen were posted on the premises and outside to maintain order.

It seems that the Christmas toy bazaar and entertainments for

children in large stores started around the mid Victorian era and
the commercial Father Christmas as we know him today made
his debut sometime during the First World War.

Christmas Cards

The custom of exchanging illustrated greetings amongst friends
on special festival days goes back to Roman and ancient
Egyptian times. Presents often had greetings inscribed upon
them.

Christmas cards have been made from cloth, celluloid,
vellum, metal, wood, clay and cork as well as the more
traditional materials such as paper or cardboard. In Victorian
times the Christmas card was often as ornate as the Valentine
card, being made out of gold leaf embossed paper, lace and satin
ribbons. The size of the greeting varied from an inscribed grain
of rice sent to the Prince of Wales in 1929 to one sent to President
Calvin Coolidge of the U.S.A. in 1924 which measured 21x33
inches.

In the fifteenth century the master engravers produced prints
which were undoubtedly the forerunner of the modern greeting
card. One of these by Master E. S. shows the Christ child with a
halo before a cross and holding a small scroll on which are the
words 'Ein quot seligior' — 'a good and happy year'.

During the eighteenth and nineteenth centuries copper plate
and wood engravers produced prints and calendars for
Christmas and the New Year mostly ordered by merchants and
trade people. These often carried advertisements and were sent
to important and revered customers in appreciation of their
patronage.

Children were often employed to colour book illustrations by
hand and some with an artistic flair prepared Christmas sheets
—illustrated single papers with space for the name of the sender
to be written in the centre. The illustrations consisted of seasonal
scenes and the sheets were on sale for few pence — the young
artists choosing street corners and markets as places to sell their
products.

Visiting cards often heavily gilded and embossed were for
some, the forerunners of the Christmas card. Many wealthy
people had Christmas visiting cards specially prepared with an
appropriate verse printed on them.

The first genuine Christmas card is generally accepted to be the one designed by J. C. Horsley in 1843 for his friend Sir Henry Cole. An edition of one thousand copies was placed on sale at Felix Summerley's Home Treasury Office in London. It was printed by lithography on stiff cardboard 5x3¼ inches in dark green sepia and hand coloured. The design shows a family party in progress beneath which are the words 'A Merry Christmas and a Happy New Year to You!' In the small panels there are pictures of people giving alms to the poor. The whole card is entwined with ivy leaves on rustic poles which act as kind of picture frame. The verse is a play on the nursery rhyme 'Old King Cole'.

To: *His good friend Cole*
        Who's a merry young soul
        And a merry young soul is he
        And may be for years to come! Hooray!

With the introduction of the penny post in 1840 and the invention of envelopes, the sending of all sorts of cards, not to mention letters, suddenly became so much easier, quicker and cheaper. Like the Valentine card, the Christmas card flourished, and its popularity increased year by year. Many greeting card publishing houses sprang up and by 1860 subjects for Christmas cards had become much more varied. Adding to the Nativity scene and the family group; robins, stage coaches, country snow scenes, candles, yule logs, holly and mistletoe and other evergreens, and even some flowers such as the Christmas rose had become popular topics for illustration. Some families preferred to send more individual cards such as photographs of themselves. Publishers introduced the comical card and the cartoon and others took up the subject of Old Father Christmas, and began a tradition for which every British child had to be thankful — the notion of the present-giving Father Christmas.

Victorians developed a craze for the mechanical or trick Christmas card. Like the Valentine card it often bore hidden messages for the eyes only of the one for whom it was intended. Most correspondence, as I mentioned in the Valentine section, was censored by strict parents trying to shield their daughters from admirers. It became the vogue for lovers to send secret messages only to be revealed by the working of a mechanical device, such as the opening of a door when a certain spot was touched, or hiding greetings under ribbons and laces. Others concealed surprises like bangs or squeaks when pressed in the right place.

Queen Mary, the grandmother of our present Queen, had a very interesting Christmas card collection which she gave to the British Museum in 1950. It is on display and includes many ingenious and mechanical cards, as well as ones sent to her by her grandchildren and made by them, including the ones signed 'Lilibet' from our present Queen.

Christmas Crackers

One of Queen Mary's cards was very elaborate containing three scenes. When the second picture was revealed it showed a pattern of roses shaped like a cracker with a hand at each end in readiness to pull it apart. In the final scene the cracker is parted to show a small silver envelope with a verse inside. It is thought to have been sent around 1870. It is sometimes thought that this card and many other trick Christmas cards were the forerunners of the Christmas cracker — that ever popular decorative addition to the Christmas table.

Apparently this is not strictly true although ideas from the Christmas cards may have been used to a certain extent. The Christmas cracker story is rather romantic and is, I think, little known in this country. Over a hundred years ago a baker in London by the name of Thomas Smith decided to take his wife on a holiday to Europe. Business was good and he felt he could leave it in safe hands for a week or two. They journeyed to France and then onto Paris. Thomas Smith was naturally very interested in the cakes and pastries made, and in particular his attention was drawn to a sweetmeat called a sugared almond, a thing unheard of in Britain at that time. These sweets were wrapped in coloured paper with each end twisted and were known as Bon-bons.

They appealed to him so much that he decided to have quantities of the sweets shipped across and sent to London where he could sell them in his shop. For a time the novelty proved a great success but after a while people began to tire of this confectionary. Smith then thought of an idea to help sell the sweets — he included a love motto in each one. This gimmick boosted sale quite considerably but he felt that the idea could be improved upon, so he substituted a small toy or novelty for the sugared almond, but this did not meet with great success. One Christmas day while watching the Yule log burning and crackling in the open grate he poked at the fire with a poker, and immediately a piece of the log burst into flame with a spurt of resin and a small bang. An idea at once flashed into his mind. Why not make a roll of paper, log shaped with a surprise crackle inside, as well as a verse and small gift? This would surely appeal to the public as no-one could resist a surprise or a bang.

The first most important task was to create a safe snap or bang when the cracker was pulled, and after many experiments Thomas Smith succeeded in producing an adequate snap or banger. He then formed the cracker as it is known today with two ends and a centre containing paper hats, mottoes, small gifts, and of course the banger.

The possibilities for decoration of such a novelty were immense, and crackers became more and more ornate and colourful with all sorts of gifts inside, some of them most expensive. The cracker was an instant success and quickly took its traditional place beside the turkey, plum pudding and mince pie.

By 1898 Thomas Smith owned a firm which produced over 13 million crackers per year, and was then the only cracker making firm in the world; British crackers were exported to all corners of the earth. Not only did the cracker trade give employment to many people in this country, but orders for different types of paper and other ingredients used in cracker and box making, stimulated trade with other countries, so helping to supply jobs for hundreds more.

Walter Smith, the son of Thomas, carried on the business with all his father's flair and expertise. His ideas for crackers included: 'Crackers from the Klondike', 'Motor Car Crackers' and 'Arctic Expedition Crackers' all reflecting notable achievements. Quite often Walter Smith was asked to produce a special order, for example a box of crackers suitable for the legal profession. He designed crackers which contained paper wigs, legal documents, a comic bill of costs and other papers written in the correct legal terms.

Usually crackers are about 12 inches (30 cms) long but of

course there have been many that have exceeded this size. For example more than once the firm has received orders asking for crackers to measure three feet (one metre) long or more — usually to house a suit of clothing as a present. Another large cracker made of wickerwork and measuring seven feet long was shown on the stage at Drury Lane theatre during a pantomime. At every performance the cracker was pulled on by two clowns and amidst a miniature explosion the cracker parted in the middle and a youngster emerged from the smoke dressed as a sprite.

The largest cracker built in the nineteenth century was over thirty feet high, and was assembled in a ballroom of a country estate in the north of England. It was built on end and had a strong wooden base, supporting a central pole and light wire lattice work forming the shape of a cracker. Strong ornate and hand painted paper covered the structure. What's more there was a complicated system of coloured electric lights with a huge detonator in the middle of the cracker. At a given signal the detonator was exploded by means of pulleys and clouds of blue and green smoke and flames poured from the cracker, and at the same time the electric lights were switched on to marvellous effect. The cracker was filled with expensive toys and sweets which were distributed to the children and adults present by ladies especially employed for the job. They reached the contents of the cracker by means of a tiny spiral staircase inside the structure!

In addition in the nineteenth century, very expensive crackers and cracker boxes were ordered — one requested by a millionaire consisted of an elegant silver casket made by an eminent firm of London Silversmiths. It contained six crackers, the wrappers of which were composed of figured satin, edged with valuable old lace. The centres were in the shape of octagonal caskets fitted with tiny silver doors and each cracker contained a valuable ring or brooch. The crackers were presented to the bridesmaids at a fashionable Christmas wedding. The cost was over £250, a considerable sum in those days.

The most expensive single cracker made in the last century was only four inches long and made in solid gold in the shape of a sheaf of wheat. A very skilled goldsmith spent six months working on the model before it was completed. It contained a ring set with rare pearls and the price then was £400.

In modern times the cracker is still as popular as ever, and although there are now many other cracker firms in production in Britain and other parts of the world, Tom Smith and Company is still the largest manufacturer. Today cracker making is often carried out by the disabled or by people working in the home. The separate parts and boxes are sent to the individuals concerned and are hand-made. People become very deft and artistic at this work and a good cracker maker can produce as many as 160,000 crackers a year.

The largest cracker ever made and recorded in the Guinness Book of Records was one which measured 42 feet in length and 7 feet in diameter, and was built in December 1972 for the Christmas showroom display of Cleales Ltd. Garage, Saffron Walden, Essex. The cracker concealed a Ford Escort car and took two weeks to build with a metal framework covered with polythene and coloured paper.

Crackers are still sometimes called Bon-bons, the French word for sweet, and when we know their history we can understand why the term is used.

CHRISTMAS CUSTOMS

Recipes
Both adults and children would enjoy working with all the spicey ingredients used in *mincemeat*. Here is a simple recipe from the *New World Radiation Cookery Book* which is also cheaper than the bought variety. The children might give away jars of mincemeat as Christmas presents.

Ingredients:

1½ lb (750 g) stoned raisins	1½ lbs (750 g) brown sugar
1 lb (500 g) candied peel	rind and juice of 1 lemon and
1 lb (500 g) sultanas	1 orange
1 lb (500 g) currants	1 oz (25 g) mixed spice
2 lbs (1 kg) apples	½ grated nutmeg
1 lb (500 g) suet	½ pint of brandy or rum
	(optional)

Mincemeat should be kept a few weeks before use so make it in November or early December.

Method. Pass the raisins, peel, half the sultanas, currants and apples twice through the mincer. If you have not got a mincer or liquidiser just chop finely by hand. Add the remainder of the fruit, suet, sugar, rind and juice of the orange and lemon, spice, nutmeg and brandy if used. Mix well and leave it in the mixing bowl for a week, well covered — and stir every day. Then turn into jam jars leaving a one inch (2½ cms) space at the top, and cover with jam pot covers.

Mince pies are not diffcult to make and also might be made by the children. If there is any pastry left over, they could make pastry dolls as children did centuries ago. They should first experiment with the pastry, finding out the best ways to make the doll shapes. Decoration for the face could include currants for eyes, peel or glacé cherries for nose and mouth and perhaps desiccated coconut could be used for hair. Other materials such as angelica might be used to decorate the body to represent clothes.

Things For Children To Make

To help keep children occupied in the waiting days before Christmas *Advent parcel calendars* could be made.

Materials needed:

2 pieces of white cardboard measuring 24x12 inches or 60x30 cms (plain coloured stiff wallpaper would suffice)

sticky tape, paints or crayons
24 small presents
wrapping paper

Method. On the piece of cardboard which is to be the front of the Advent calendar children should draw and colour a large all-over scene — something associated with Christmas. When this is dry they should then draw, in a haphazard fashion, 24 squares measuring 1½ inches (4 cms) on each side over the painted scene. They then cut round three sides of the squares leaving one side to be folded to make a small door. Next place the identical piece of cardboard underneath and draw the 1½ inches (4 cms) square doors in exactly the same position. The top cardboard should then be removed and the squares cut round on the undersheet only leaving the hinge at the bottom so that the squares make ledges. Wrap up 24 small presents — nuts, sweets, coloured marbles, rings etc. and attach one with sticky tape to the back of each flap on the under sheet. Then close up the flaps so that the cardboard is flat once more. Decorate the flaps with a small Christmas item such as a robin, candle, Christmas stocking, etc. Hinge the two sheets together at the top with sticky tape. Number the doors on the front sheet in any order from 1 to 24 but keeping the last — the 24 — for the centre. When the last door is opened the picture seen is usually the Nativity scene.

Starting on 1 December the children take it in turns to open the appropriate door, see the picture inside and then pull down the flap to receive the present.

A Kissing Bush is easy to prepare and makes an interesting addition to the Christmas scene.

Children can either make a bush by tying some evergreens together, dipping them in white flour paste and leaving them to dry before decorating and hanging up, or they can make a more permanent base to keep from year to year.

For a wire based bush two hoops of wire will be needed, or small hula or bowling hoops made out of wood or plastic would be ideal. One circle stands at right angles to the other and they are fixed by string to form horizontal and vertical rings. The hoops should then be covered with coloured paper or streamers. Pick strands of ivy, holly, pieces of fir and laurel, in fact any evergreen that is available. The greens can be treated as described in the May Day section to prolong their life over Christmas. The evergreens should be attached in an attractive way to cover the hoops. Rosy apples, small oranges and mandarins, tinsel, baubles and small gifts can all be hung on the bush as was the custom in the past. A small piece of mistletoe if available could be hung in the centre. All that remains to be done is to hang the bush in a prominent position.

For an unusual table decoration *Christingles* could be made by the children.

Materials needed:

2 or 3 large oranges	pieces of red ribbon
2 or 3 small candles	dates, figs, large raisins and
small plates to provide a firm	monkey nuts in shells
base	cocktail sticks

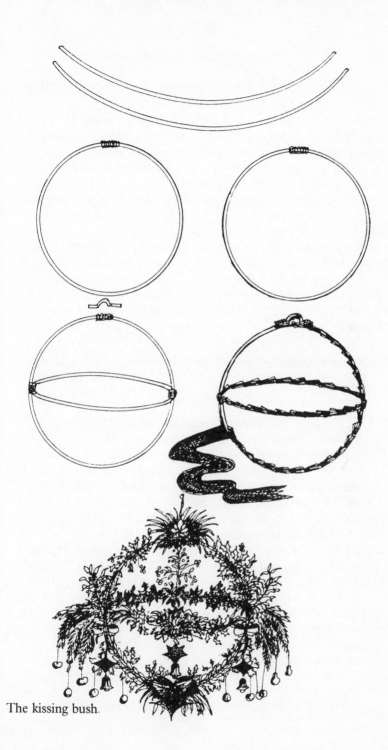

The kissing bush.

Method. Cut off a flat piece of orange peel from the base of the orange so that it stands firmly on the base without wobbling. Cut a hole into the top of the orange big enough to wedge the end of the candle in firmly. Next stick cocktail sticks all around the orange and place nuts and dried fruits on the ends — porcupine fashion. Lastly tie the red ribbon around the centre of the orange. Make the others in a similar manner. Christingles, when spaced out on the table with the candles lit look attractive and unusual.

Christmas Cards

Here are some ideas for novelty *Christmas cards* that children could try.

Father Christmas card.

Materials needed:

pieces of stiff card or paper
either white or pastel coloured
measuring approximately
6x15 inches (15x38) cms)

glue or sticky tape
cotton wool
wooden lolly stick
piece of red or yellow
cellophane

Fold the card into three so that it measures 5x6 inches (13x15 cms). Cut off one section, and this will be used for the Father Christmas on the chimney.

The other folded piece forms the main Christmas card, with the fold at the top. Measure down 1 inch (2½ cms) from the fold, draw a line and cut off a slanting piece at each end to make the roof shape of the house. The roof will then be 1 inch (2½ cms) deep, and still folded at the top.

On the other piece of paper draw and colour a small figure of Father Christmas and a chimney just a bit wider than the figure so that he will have room to go down it — say a chimney about 2 inches (5 cms) wide. Colour the chimney as if it was made of red bricks. Colour the house shape on the large card, drawing tiles on the roof, bricks on the walls, and doors and windows. Cut out squares for windows and stick on the inside pieces of red or yellow cellophane which will make the house look as if it has a light inside. Stick the chimney pot onto the front side of the fold in the roof, so that it rises above the roof. Next cut a slit in the fold of the roof as wide as the chimney and just behind it. This is

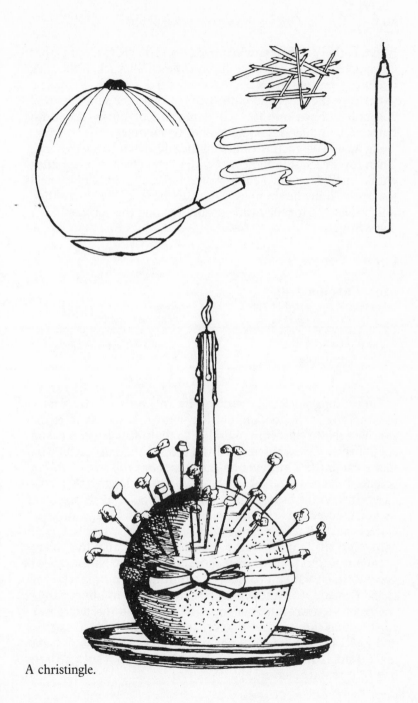

A christingle.

where Father Christmas will move up and down. Cut out Father Christmas and stick him on the end of the lolly stick. If the stick is too big use two strips of cardboard stuck together to make a stick. Push the other end of the stick through the slit in the roof and pull it down into the centre of the Christmas card, until Father Christmas is hidden behind the chimney. To show him going up and down, push and pull the stick from inside the card. Then cover each side of the roof with a layer of cotton wool stuck with a little glue to make it look like snow, and this will conceal the place where the chimney is stuck to the roof. The card is then finished except for the inside decoration and the verse, which I deal with later.

Cracker Christmas card.

Materials needed:

a piece of cardboard or stiff paper measuring 8x12 inches (20x30 cms)

small present

a cardboard centre or a toilet roll

pieces of coloured crepe and cellophane paper

2 push through paper clips

glue, cotton, crayons, or felt tips

tissue paper for hats

On the long side of the cardboard with a ruler find the centre and mark it at the top and bottom. Next fold the edges of the shorter sides to the centre marking so that the edges meet. You should then have a three sided stand up Christmas card. Next make the cracker by covering the cardboard roll with a roll of coloured crepe paper 4 inches (10 cms) longer than the cardboard centre. Stick with glue or fix with sticky tape, and then make a cracker shape by tying a knot at each end of the roll with cotton, and pull tight, leaving about a 2 inch (5cms) frill at each end. Cut the paper at the edges to make the frill more pronounced. Decorate the rest of the cracker with more coloured paper. Press each end of the cracker until the normal cracker shape is made. Cut the whole cracker in half and fit it to the centre of the front edges of the card with push through paper clips, taking care that the cracker meets in the middle exactly, and looks like a whole cracker when the card is closed. Next make a small fringe or decoration to cover the join, sticking it to one side of the cracker only.

The inside of the card will convey what happens when the cracker is pulled. Directly on the inside paint or colour a large 'blob' to denote the 'bang' when the card is opened. Print 'BANG' in large letters over the blob. Underneath supply a cracker motto or riddle, such as, 'What can a blind man always see?' answer — 'A good joke'.

Wrap up a small present and push it down one end of the cracker roll. Make a paper hat, crown or dunce-shaped out of tissue paper, and roll it up and put it in the other side of the cracker roll. Decorate the inside of the card, write a Christmas verse and sign your name.

Lucky bird hat Christmas card.

Materials needed:

piece of card or stiff paper measuring approximately 8x12 inches (20x30 cms)

2 push through paper clips pieces of coloured tissue paper, glue, crayons

First draw a one inch (2½ cms) border along the top and bottom of the long sides of the paper. Decorate this border with robins, holly, bells and candles.

Next fold the card so that it measures 6x8 inches (15x20 cms) and stands like a normal Christmas card, with the coloured borders showing on the front and back.

In the centre of the front fold of the card draw a tree stump coming out of the bottom border, and then draw a large bird sitting on it, so large that it nearly touches the sides of the paper. Draw his body, head, beak, tail and feet — on the stump. Next colour in his beak, eyes and feet and outline the rest of the shape in black. Tear the coloured tissue paper into small pieces, twisting them so that the middle comes to a point. Dab some glue lightly over the bird shape, and then stick the pieces of tissue paper, the more colours the better, all over the bird, by the pointed pieces in the middle. Let the edges of each small piece stick out and give the impression of bushy feathers. Make a tail by sticking on strips of tissue paper. Children must be careful not to use too much glue as this will spoil the whole effect. Decorate the rest of the card inside with Christmas scenes and verses. The card can also be turned into a hat by cutting off the top border and fastening it at each end of the bottom border, with the two paper clips.

As mentioned earlier the lucky bird was a symbol of good luck and happiness for people years ago.

Christmas Card Verses

Verses on Christmas cards are usually so simple that children could compose their own, especially if they include in the verse the name of the person to whom they are sending the card. Here are a few ideas:

Christmas has brought the Lucky Bird,
He has a song which must be heard;
Good luck is mixed with Christmas cheer,
That will be with you all the year.

You think the card is arty?
Then give three cheers most hearty!
And come and join the party,
At this Christmas time.

Brightly glows the holly,
Come in Mike and Molly,
Let us all be jolly,
This is Christmas time.

We must not be sparing –
For old folks be caring,
Gifts and joys be sharing,
All at Christmas time.

Christmas cards are posted —
Beef and turkey roasted;
The family health is toasted,
This is Christmas time.

Snow is on the hedges,
And on the window ledges,
Children get your sledges,
This is Christmas time!

Here is a poem describing Christmas a hundred years ago, and published in *Punch* magazine. We could still use some of the verses today:

> *Icicles and frost and snow;*
> *Holly green and mistletoe;*
> *Hasty kisses,*
> *Stolen blisses,*
> *Blushing misses, whispers low.*
>
> *Blazing fires within the grates,*
> *Lads and lasses on their skates;*
> *Careless sliding,*
> *Graceful gliding,*
> *Pairs colliding, broken pates.*
>
> *Laughter which unceasing flows;*
> *Welcome, whereso'er it goes;*
> *Slipp'ry places,*
> *Footstep traces,*
> *Glowing faces, frozen toes.*
>
> *Nipping breezes from the hills;*
> *Robins upon window sills;*
> *Toil forsaking,*
> *Pudding making,*
> *Pastry baking, Christmas bills.*

Nativity Scenes

Many children would enjoy making a nativity stand-up scene to decorate a window ledge or shelves at Christmas time.

For the back cloth and floor you will need sheets of stiff paper or cardboard — stiff plainish wallpaper would be ideal. For the cutouts the cardboard from cereal packets would do, and crayons or paints, glue or sticky tape, and other items which I will describe later.

I was thinking of three scenes, but of course these can be varied. The baby in a manger with Mary and Joseph in the stable with perhaps an ox or ass or cow as well. The shepherds on the hillside, looking up at the angel bringing them the good news of

Nativity scene.

the birth of Christ, and in this scene you could add sheep, and
bushes and perhaps an imitation fire. And the three wise men in
the desert following the star, riding on camels.

For *the stable scene* paint both sides of a large piece of
cardboard or stiff paper measuring 24x8 inches (60x20cms),
brown would be a suitable colour. When dry fold 6 inches (15
cms) in from each end of the long side, making a three sided
room. Then cut a piece of cardboard for the floor, 14x7 inches
(35x18 cms) and paint it. When dry measure an inch (2½ cms) on
three sides of the cardboard — both short sides and one of the
long sides. Draw a line along each of these sides an inch (2½ cms)
in from the edge. Next cut up to the line with inch (2½ cms) wide
cuts so that it looks rather like a frill. Dab some glue on the cut
pieces, and glue to the back and sides of the stand-up part to
make the floor, by folding and sticking the cut parts onto the
outside edges of the upright.

Paint lines on the background to look like the struts in the
stable walls.

Draw and paint the figures of Mary and Joseph on the cereal
cardboard, Joseph is usually portrayed as standing and Mary

sitting. Draw fairly large tabs, to bend back and stick to the floor to make the figures stand upright. Cut out Joseph, and Mary, and paint a match box for Mary to sit on, and bend her body into a sitting position, so that she looks comfortable. Next make the manger by covering another match box and painting it. Insert used matches for legs. Draw any animals suitable for the stable, not forgetting the large tabs under their feet to stick down when ready. When the figures have been coloured and cut out, the children can then arrange them in the stable in group form and then stick them down by the tabs onto the floor. Straw or dried grass could be strewn on the floor and a little put into the manger. A small celluloid doll wrapped in swaddling clothes (narrow strips of bandages) could be put in the manger. If the children wished they might add clothes of material to the cut out figures.

The shepherds' scene would need the same sort of background as the nativity scene, but the sky should be dark to show night time. The centre piece could be a fire made out of red cellophane paper and twigs, and to make it more effective a small lighted torch could be hidden in the centre. Four or five shepherds, some standing, some sitting and some lying, but all with their heads looking upwards could be drawn, coloured and cut out and stuck down with tabs around the fire. Some could be carrying crooks, and sheep might be in the picture too. The angel, suspended by black cotton from the 'sky' should be a figure dressed in white with angel wings at the back and a slight yellow haze surrounding it. Bushes and small rocks could be added to make the scene more realistic.

The Three Kings scene in the desert, following the star should be made in a similar manner. Using the same background formula, paint the sky dark with dark brown sand dunes in the distance. Glue the floor and then cover with sand, shaking off the surplus. Either the children could draw camels and cut them out to stick on with the tabs, or, if preferred, horses. The three kings should be dressed in bright clothes and made to look as Eastern as possible with beards and turbans and flowing robes. The star should be cut out of silver paper and suspended by black cotton to hang in the 'sky'. A few palm trees and rocks coloured, cut out and stuck on with tabs will complete the scene.

The Three Kings.

NEW YEAR'S EVE — 31 DECEMBER

When we think of the last day of the year and the customs associated with it, many of us conjure up a mental picture of Old Father Time complete with long grey hair, beard and sickle gradually fading out and a new babe fresh and unspoilt being ushered into this world. In Guernsey children used to make a mock figure of Old Father Time on this day and after parading him round the streets bury him in the sands on the sea shore. This ceremony was described as 'enterrer le vieux bout de l'an.'

Years ago the bells rang out all over the country and signified the ringing out of the bad and the ringing in of the new. An old verse describing the scene went as follows:

> *For Hope shall brighten days to come*
> *A memory gild the past!*
> *Bells ring out the old and bad —*
> *And ring in the new and good.*

The explanations as to the derivation of the word Hogmanay are many and varied. To the pious English in days gone by the word Hogmanay meant something crude and vulgar — attributed to the way the festival was celebrated in Scotland. Not without good reason was it called the 'Daft Days', and in France, which had close ties with Scotland in the past, the first day of the New Year was called the Fool's Festival.

It is known that the Druids went into the woods at this time of year and picked sprigs of mistletoe for people to wear and hang up in their dwellings as protection against evil influences. The phrase 'Au gui menez' — 'to the mistletoe go', was chanted by French beggars in Scotland in the sixteenth century as they burst in on church services held on the last day of the year. The beggars were called Bachettes or Guisards and their cry went as follows, 'Au gui menez, Rollet, Follet, tin, lin, mainte du blanc et point du bis.' The Scots translated it as follows — Hogmanay, Trololay, Give us your white bread and none of your grey.'

In time people took up the custom and went from house to house crying for Hogmanay bread and cheese. Children used to sing this quaint verse outside houses of the rich on Old Year's Night:

> *Get up good wife and shake your feathers*
> *And dinna think that we are beggars,*
> *For we are bairns come out to play*
> *Get up and gie's our hogmanay*

Sometimes children called this Nog-money.

The month of December in the North of England and Scotland has been known as Hagmena from early times and comes from the Greek meaning 'holy moon'. A Christian interpretation of the word Hogmanay is again taken from the French, 'Homme est ne — Trois Rois la.' Translated it reads, 'A Man is born — Three Kings are here, marking the coming of the Three Kings after the birth of Christ.

Whatever the history, the Scots regard this festival as the most important. In years gone by hundreds of people would gather in the market places all over the country to listen for the peal of bells which welcomed the New Year. Then the community would work themselves up into a joyous frenzy — drinking, dancing and making merry to the skirl of bagpipes in the background. In Glasgow the boats and ships on the Clyde would sound their hooters and sirens to add to the pandemonium. In Edinburgh crowds would gather outside Tron Kirk and when the clock sounded midnight the revelries would begin. After a while the crowds would disperse a little and the first footing would start. This consisted of young people visiting their friends and relatives where they would be welcomed with lavish supplies of whisky and food. The first foot had to be a tall dark man who carried a piece of coal and a piece of cake or black bun into the house. This symbolised warmth and food for the occupants for the coming year. A black bun was a piece of rich fruit cake with a pastry base. If the first footers were barred from a house they would tramp around the building stamping their feet to shake the dust off their shoes, as they regarded it as bad luck to bring that dust into the next house. Women were never allowed in first as this was regarded as a bad luck sign, but the women had other tasks to do; they always polished their silver on the last day of the old year to bring luck and make a clean start to the new year. In some parts of Scotland women would not sweep their houses from noon on 31 December until noon of New Year's Day for fear of sweeping out the good luck. In Scotland the first footing goes on all night until every house in the neighbourhood has been visited, and the Scots have two Bank holidays to recover from this celebration.

In the rest of Britain the festivities on New Year's Eve are carried out in the same manner but not so heartily; Christmas being the main festival of the year south of the border. Nevertheless most Britons have parties or stay up with friends to see the New Year in and the first foot customs are observed in the same manner.

Centuries ago people went a-wassailing on New Year's Eve. This custom was similar to the Hogmanay ritual of going from house to house asking for food in Scotland, but had the added attraction of the wassailing bowl. This was usually made of wood, decorated with greenery and ribbons and contained ale, roasted apples, toast, nutmeg and sugar. The idea was that if the wassailers sang a song outside a house of their choice and offered the inhabitants a sip out of their wassailing bowl, then they should receive gifts of food or money. An old wassailing song went like this:

> *Good master, at your door,*
> *Our wassail we begin;*
> *We all are maidens poor,*
> *So we pray you let us in*
> *And drink our wassail.*
> *All hail! Wassail!*
> *Wassail! Wassail!*

The tradition of the wassail bowl is an old one and it is known that in the early days of the church the monasteries possessed a wassailing bowl which was filled at this time of year and everyone from the Abbot to the poorest servant had a sip from it.

A very old custom was for people to go a-wassailing to apple orchards on Old Year's Night, a ritual which is definitely pagan in its origin. One tree in the orchard would be picked out and the company would pray for a good apple crop, sing wassailing songs, drink hot cider and pour some over the roots of the tree, and make as much noise as possible with tin lids and bird scarers to ward off evil spirits which may be lurking to damage the apple harvest. In Sussex this night was called Apple Howling after the lines in the wassailing song, 'Stand fast root, bear well crop, Pray God send us a good howling crop.'

The burning of the 'Clavie' at a village called Burghead on the southern shore of the Moray Firth was carried out on every Hogmanay. Sailors would prepare a specially made tar barrel using no metal, and carry it around when lighted, on their backs amid the cheers of the villagers. The melted tar would run down their backs and burn them and if the carrier stumbled he could expect to die before the New Year was out. After several men had taken turns the barrel was set on a hill called Doorie and it rolled down, blazing all the way. People thought it was lucky if they caught a burning brand from it to light their fires. This custom has its origins in the mists of time and may have some connection with the way wrong doers were put to death.

The giving of gifts on New Year's Eve and New Year's Day was very popular. People wanted to prolong the feeling of friendliness and togetherness experienced when the New Year was welcomed in, and the gifts themselves were symbols of good wishes extended to family and friends. Children would give gifts of oranges or lemons stuck with cloves, to their God-parents, asking for their blessing. Capons were often given, and royalty seems to have done especially well receiving presents from subjects craving favour. In modern times the gift giving custom has been discontinued but the sentiment behind the deed is remembered every time we wish someone, 'A Happy New Year.'

What the future held was most important to people long ago, partly because life then was very precarious. A common practice at this time of year was to open the Bible haphazardly and point to a verse with eyes closed. The message contained in the verse would then predict the fortune of the person concerned. Shepherds used to say that if the morning of New Year's Day showed a red sky then it meant strife amongst the leaders of the land, and many robberies. In some parts of the country girls would drop a little white of egg into a cup of water which would make the shape of an initial; it was thought they would eventually marry a person bearing the same initial.

But apart from these divinations people were sensible enough to realise that the only way to improve the quality of life was to indulge in a little soul searching and self analysis, and the beginning of a new year was the ideal time to start. New Year resolutions have been made for centuries, and here is a list recorded in Hone's Year Book in 1832:

> *Never put off till tomorrow what you can do today.*
> *Never trouble another for what you can do yourself.*
> *Never spend your money before you have it.*
> *Never buy what you do not want because it is*
> *cheap; it will be dear to you.*
> *Pride costs more than hunger, thirst and cold.*
> *We never repent of having eaten too little.*
> *Nothing is troublesome that we do willingly.*
> *How much pain have cost us the evils which have*
> *never happened.*

In the first few minutes of the New Year when in the genial company of family and friends men and women experience a feeling of happiness and hopefulness and regard the New Year as a chance for a new beginning. There is a lifting of the spirit and a feeling of freedom from the troubles and worries of the past. It is this possession of steadfastness and faith which has enabled man to survive through plague and war, through fire, flood and famine right through the ages. Throughout the centuries festivals and feast days have given purpose and cheer to everyday life.

ACKNOWLEDGEMENTS

I would like to thank the following people and institutions for providing me with valuable and often rare information which has helped to produce a book which shows, I hope, an original slant on the festivals and customs which are still part of our daily lives.

Len Strasman, Ian and Dorothy Brown, John Clark, Alison Adburgham, all librarians who have worked so diligently for me in this country and in America, *Punch* Magazine, The John Lewis Partnership and especially the archivist Mrs. Lorna Poole, Tom Smith Crackers (Norwich) and many others. Some of the information contained in the three volumes of *British Calendar Customs* edited by A. R. Wright and T. E. Lones, has been invaluable in my research, as was *The History of the Christmas Card* by George Buday and *An Egg at Easter* by Venetia Newall. Marian McNeill's book *Hallowe'en* and the recipes therein provided an insight into Scottish customs hitherto unknown to a Sassenach like myself.

BIBLIOGRAPHY

Benedictine Monks ed., *The Book of Saints* (fifth edition), Adam & Charles Black (1966).

Brand, John, *Observations on the Popular Antiquities of Great Britain*, Henry Bohn (London, 1849).

Brody, Alan, *The English Mummers and their Plays*, Routledge & Kegan Paul (London, 1971).

Buday, George, *The History of the Christmas Card*, Spring Books (London, 1954).

Chambers, R. ed., *The Book of Days*, W. R. Chambers (London and Edinburgh).

Feasey, Lynette, *Old England at Play*, George Harrap (1943).

Franklin, Alexander, *Seven Miracle Plays*, Oxford University Press (1963).

Hole, Christina, *Christmas and its Customs*, Richard Bell (1956).

Hone, William, *The Every-day Book*, William Hone (London, 1826).

Hone, William, *The Year Book*, William Hone (London, 1832).

James, E. O., *Seasonal Feasts and Festivals*, Thames & Hudson, (1961).

Jamieson, John, *Jamieson's Scottish Dictionary, Volume 2 — Paisley*, Alexander Gardner (1880).

Keighley, David, *Corn Dollies*, Photo Precision Ltd (St. Ives, Huntingdon).

Lambeth, M., *Straw Craft: More Golden Dollies*, John Baker (1974).

McNeill, F. Marian, *The Silver Bough Volume III*, William Maclellan (Glasgow, 1961).

McNeill, F. Marian, *Hallowe'en: its Origins, Rites and Ceremonies in the Scottish Tradition*, Albyn Press (1970).

Munt, Bert, *Bonfire*, Pamphlet unpublished 1958 in Lewes Library.

Newall, Venetia, *An Egg at Easter*, Routledge & Kegan Paul (1971).

O'Halloran, Simon, *Bonfires in Lewes*, Pamphlet unpublished in Lewes Library.

White, Florence, *Good Things in England*, Cape.

Wright, A. R. and Lones T. E. ed., *British Calendar Customs Volumes 1, 2 and 3*, published for the Folk-lore Society by William Glaisher (1940).